"As I read this book, I thought—*it's about time!* And frankly, I couldn't put it down. I lost track of the times I said, 'What?' or 'Wow!' Tim is real, relatable, unfailingly honest—a breath of fresh air in what is often a stale Christian publishing culture. This is about character development instead of image management! It's about time."

–Ray Johnston, Senior Pastor of Bayside Church

"Tim outlines the simplicity and complexity of being marked by love, and why it should be the hallmark of those of us who follow Jesus. I'm so grateful for Tim's voice and for this book."

–Carey Nieuwhof, Author and Founding Pastor
of Connexus Church

"For the last thirty years of pastoring churches and studying the Bible, I have looked for the core message that all others center around. My good friend, Tim Stevens, has found it. While I have benefited from everything that Tim has written over the years, this book has the greatest potential to really change a life, a family, a neighborhood...the entire world. Tim is about to take you on a wonderful, authentic ride. Enjoy the journey; embrace the invitation to be marked by love."

–Randy Frazee, Pastor and Author
of *What Happens After You Die*

"The game has changed for sharing faith. Old methods are out, and it's time for a new approach. I've had the privilege of working alongside Tim for several years now. Watching how he works, treats people, and mirrors Jesus in life, I can attest that he lives a life marked by love. I can't think of anyone better suited to help reshape the conversation about sharing faith than Tim. Read this book, and you'll be better prepared for the new day that is dawning."

–William Vanderbloemen, Founder and CEO
of Vanderbloemen Search Group

MARKED BY LOVE

A DARE TO WALK AWAY FROM
JUDGMENT AND HYPOCRISY

TIM STEVENS

SHILOH RUN PRESS
An Imprint of Barbour Publishing, Inc.

Published in association with The Blythe Daniel Agency, P.O. Box 64197, Colorado Springs, CO 80962-4197.

Cover Design: Greg Jackson, Thinkpen Design

Published by Shiloh Run Press, an imprint of Barbour Publishing, Inc., 1810 Barbour Drive, Uhrichsville, Ohio 44683, www.shilohrunpress.com

Our mission is to inspire the world with the life-changing message of the Bible.

Member of the
Evangelical Christian
Publishers Association

Printed in the United States of America.

CONTENTS

Introduction 9

1. Heart Surgery in a Cornfield 15

2. I'm Tired of the Mask 19

3. Tattoos & Traditions 24

4. The Time God Spoke 30

5. Famous Last Words 35

6. I Don't Want to Be Called a Christian 42

7. Lessons in a White Pickup Truck 48

8. Bob's Simple Question 53

9. The Channels between the Channels 58

10. A 200-Pound Bag of Sewage 62

11. Jesus as Jewelry 69

12. Stop Talking and Start Loving 76

13. A Chinese Massage 83

14. Happy Holidays 91

15. The Next Person 98

16. Who Is My Neighbor? 103

17. The Principle of Proximity 109

18. Three Girls and a Rumor 113

19. It's a Fact 123

20. The Day a Punk Taught Me about Love 127

21. People Don't Care How Much You Know 135

22. There's More to Life Than Green Grass 145

23. A World of "Us vs. Them" 155

24. Kill 'Em with Kindness 164

25. Tess Ran Away 173

26. He Gives and Takes Away. Or Does He? 177

27. The Day I Tried to Buy a Car 185

28. A Story of Love from an Unlikely Source 191

29. The Passenger in Row 20 197

30. You Are Loved 204

31. It's the Only Thing That Matters 208

Notes 215

DEDICATION

To my dad:

He was a man who showed me how to love every day.

As I watched him love my mom, sacrificially giving of himself to her, never raising a voice in anger for fifty-eight years of marriage, I learned how to love my wife.

I watched him lead and serve his coworkers well as a businessman for decades—and I learned what a true servant leader looks like.

I watched Dad help widows, neighbors, friends, and family—he taught me what it looks like to put others' needs above my own.

I saw him treat everyone with respect, refusing to gossip or slander or judge someone because they were different.

Dad faithfully lived a life marked by love for seventy-seven years. His legacy lives on in my life and the words I've written in this book.

ROSS STEVENS
1942–2018

INTRODUCTION

Have you read the news? Have you seen the headlines? The world is a mess. It is chaotic and frazzled and sometimes evil and unfair. Abuse is rampant— against women, against children, against those who appear weak. The trafficking of humans has never been higher. Right here in America, men and women are dying alone in the streets because they don't have the means to provide for themselves or access basic medical care.

World leaders, who are supposed to be leading us to a more peaceful place, taunt each other with threats of nuclear destruction. Political leaders use social media to destroy the reputations of those with whom they disagree—this happens so often it no longer surprises us. Sides are polarized and hate oozes out of people on all extremes as they verbally undress and then skin and gut their opponents.

But it's not just politics. The ugliness, judgment, and insult-slinging hit much closer to home.

Many of us daily show up at workplaces filled with dishonesty, jealousy, backstabbing, competitiveness, and gossip. Employees in many companies still experience discrimination, and qualified people are not given opportunities to advance because of their age, gender, race, or lifestyle.

Families all around us ooze with hate and bitterness as

they deal with the dysfunction that has plagued their family for generations. Statements like "I wish you were dead" and "I never want to see you again" are all too common in these settings.

Our churches aren't immune either. We love to draw lines and boxes to define who is "in" and who is "out." We fight over songs and potlucks and buildings and even what we will call ourselves. It gets to the point where we can no longer stand each other, so we split and go our own way. People who used to worship together can no longer even pass one another in the aisle at Walmart without seething anger bubbling up and out.

But it's not just our churches or our workplaces or the families around us.

And it's not only our world leaders and institutions.

It's even closer yet.

It's in *me*.

I struggle to be loving. At times, I want to lash out. I have judgmental thoughts about other people, and sometimes my thoughts are even hateful. I struggle to forgive others when I am hurt. I have a hard time loving people who are belligerent or obnoxious.

Recently, I was driving to my office. I was late, traffic was unusually heavy, and it seemed like all the people around me were driving like idiots. I had just finished the manuscript for this book, *Marked by Love*. Do you see the irony?

A woman passed me going too fast and cut in front of me too soon. I flashed my lights and laid on the horn. I was mad. She had violated my space. Who did she think she was? I pressed on the accelerator and followed her way too closely, just to prove my point. For the next few minutes, I kept maneuvering and waiting for the opportunity to do the same thing to her that she had just done to me. Finally, I pulled up beside her, ready to communicate my displeasure. I'm not quite sure what I expected, but she looked like a really nice lady and didn't even glance in my direction.

About twenty minutes later, the lane I was in was slowing down ahead, so I quickly changed lanes. The guy behind me, whom I cut off a bit too closely, laid on his horn and flashed his lights. He was obviously unhappy. I smiled and waved, just to pour fuel on his raging fire of emotions. I knew why he was mad. I knew what I had just done—and yet I somehow felt smug and more justified than the woman who had done the same thing to me just moments before.

In those moments when I'm driving and running late, I don't like the me who emerges. I don't like the thoughts that form in my head about the people in the cars around me—fellow human beings with lives and families and dreams. I'm not proud of the words I speak.

I tell you this story to let you know—I am flawed. I have not yet arrived. I have not nailed down this thing called love. I'm not the guy who put his selfishness in a suitcase long ago and now thinks only about others.

I am a fellow human on the journey of life.

You might think the guy who writes a book called *Marked by Love* is likely a big hugger. He's probably a guy who is so warm and fuzzy that everyone walks away from him saying, "Wow, he is so loving!"

That would describe my wife, not me. I am not antisocial, but I'm a bit of an introvert. I don't mind hugs, but I'm pretty awkward at initiating them. I've tried everything I can to develop a warm personality and have made some progress—but not much more than someone jumping on a trampoline has made progress in shooting himself to the moon.

This book doesn't come from my personality. It doesn't come from a ton of "look how loving I am" stories. You aren't going to get to the end of this book and wish you could be more like me when you grow up.

This is a passion project. *Marked by Love* is my seventh published book. The first six were all about leadership—sharing practical skills from what I have learned in the environments where I led and from the people who surrounded me. I enjoyed writing each one and believe they continue to add value. (Really, go buy one. Or two. Or six.) I'm still very interested in helping leaders grow.

But this is different. I began writing *Marked by Love* more than six years ago. It has taken me ten times longer to finish this book than any of the others. Every book prior to this one came from my head, but this one comes from my heart. The content has come from the deepest parts of me and has picked up speed and passion as it has surfaced. It is the rumination of a fifty-year-old man trying to make sense of what he believes. Of what he can do to make the world a better place.

You see, the older I get, the less certain I am about a lot of things:

- Are my conservative views about financial and economic issues right? I don't know.

- Are my progressive views about immigration, war, or other social issues correct? Maybe. Maybe not.

- Was the earth really created in six twenty-four-hour days? I can't say for sure—I wasn't there.

- Is there really a lake of fire called hell? As far as I know, no one has ever seen it and come back to talk about it. So maybe?

- Will people really fly out of cemeteries when Jesus comes back? Uh, maybe?

- Are churches that dunk you under the water more right than those who sprinkle? That's a can of worms.

- Should women be able to preach? Not touching that one.

I believe a lot of things. But am I right? I don't know. Many of these issues have become nonissues to me. Others can argue about them. Others can spend years debating and studying and writing books about postmodern epistemology, religious pluralism, or the end times.

But those things won't change the world.

Spoiler alert: Throughout this book, I aim to convince you that love was the common theme of Jesus' life. I'm here to tell you that you can study all you want, you can know Greek and Hebrew, you can win every religious argument—but if you aren't becoming more loving in the process, then it is all worthless.

If you aren't living a life marked by love, then you are missing the point.

We can build churches, train choirs, preach sermons, and educate people in theology, but if our members aren't becoming disciples who are marked by love, then why are we doing it?

I want to convince you that the one ingredient that can make a difference in the hallways of Congress, in schools, in workplaces, in churches, in homes, and in personal hearts is love. When you and I run every action, thought, reaction, word, and core belief through a filter of love, then we will change the world.

Before you begin, I have one request. You need to relax. Don't work too hard. Don't take notes. This isn't a how-to manual. You aren't going to find discussion questions at the end of each chapter. This is not the typical linear, step-by-step guide that provides quick solutions.

Just take it a chapter at a time. Let each story build to the finish. I'm not going to slowly build a case with thirty steps leading to a climactic conclusion. Rather, I'm going to ask you to consider whether you are marked by love in thirty different ways. So ride the waves. Take the journey with me—back and forth, up and down. Don't overthink it. Just let the words take root in your heart and mind as you read.

I really believe this is it. Love—it *is* all that matters. The entire game is won or lost in how well we love others.

Let's journey together.

1
HEART SURGERY IN A CORNFIELD

I was born in Kansas and lived in Chicago for a year or so, but I did most of my growing up in Pleasant Hill, a suburb of Des Moines, Iowa. Pleasant Hill was exactly what it sounds like—a small town of pleasantly rolling hills and large yards in neighborhoods, intermixed with cornfields and forests.

Our house was in a new area on Ash Drive, and I just knew it was going to be the perfect place for an adventurous kid to explore. I knew this even before we moved, because one day, as our split-level home was being built, we visited the construction site. The opportunities for mischief were way too inviting. My parents turned their backs, and before they could blink, I jumped out of the upper floor living-room window cut-outs, not yet filled with glass, into a huge snow pile in the front yard. After an initial moment of panic, they saw the fun I was having and let me jump what must have been a hundred more times.

That was symbolic of the years that followed. My friend and I built bike ramps and paths in the forest across the street behind his house. Down the street was a stream and pond that brought hours of fun. In my backyard was an old-growth forest that ran behind all the houses on our street, and beyond that a cornfield. We had hideouts and tree houses and defined territories that we "ruled" in our make-believe kingdoms. In the spring, we spent time in the forests, and in the summer and fall, we played for hours in the cornfields.

Paul Blakely was a year younger than me. He had just moved to a house on my street, and we went to the same school. Paul and I did everything together. We would race home from school, do our homework as fast as we could, and head outside and play until dark. In the summertime, without the obstacle of school, we could easily spend six or eight hours a day playing together. We would get so wrapped up that some days we'd forget to come home for lunch.

Paul looked up to me. It wasn't just that I was older but because I had more friends and was a bit more wired socially. We were probably both nerds, but perhaps I was less of one. I just remember sensing that he admired me.

And that's why I felt so bad one particular day.

We had been playing in the cornfield, just goofing off and talking about life (or whatever fourth graders talk about). It was between harvest and planting, so we had several acres of dirt in which to play. We had some little shovels with us, and we were digging holes and just goofing off. That's when I spotted a bulldozer parked off in the distance. A new street was being built, and the bulldozer was sitting at the edge of the cornfield behind the new road.

Ever since I was little, I had been fascinated by construction sites and big trucks and tractors. I guess every little boy is. On this day, my curiosity led us over to the bulldozer. I hopped on and goofed around in the driver's seat. I wanted so badly to start it and move some dirt. What would be cooler than that?

That's when I noticed the keys in the ignition. I turned the key expecting to hear the engine scream to life. Nothing.

I tried everything. I couldn't figure out how to start the bull-dozer. My dreams for digging a giant hole were slipping away.

That's when I got an idea. If I couldn't drive this bulldozer, no one else could either. I took the keys out of the ignition, jumped off the bulldozer, and walked a few hundred feet out into the barren cornfield.

Paul followed and, seeing the keys dangling in my hand, asked, "What are you doing? Where are you going? Why do you have the keys?"

I stopped and took my little shovel and started digging. I dug a hole about twelve inches deep, dropped the keys in the hole, and filled it back up with dirt. All the while, Paul begged me to stop. He told me I shouldn't do it, asked what I was thinking, and warned me we were going to get in trouble.

I didn't care. I didn't listen. I just buried the keys and walked away.

It was nearly dark, so we walked quietly back to our homes. Paul didn't say anything else. The silence was deafening.

That night, I cried myself to sleep. I felt so guilty, so aware of the blackness of my heart. I couldn't understand myself. I could still hear Paul pleading with me to stop and my refusal to listen. I played the day over and over in my head, and with each rewind I grew more disgusted with myself and saddened at my terrible choices.

The next afternoon I got off the school bus, and as soon as I could get permission to go outside and play, I headed straight for the cornfield. I spent hours looking for the spot where I'd buried those keys. I had my shovel with me again and dug up dozens of locations, desperately trying to find the keys and undo my wrong. Tears, mixed with dirt, streamed down my face, but I never found the keys. I couldn't undo my sin.

Every afternoon for days, I would head out to the cornfield and resume my search for the keys. By then, the bulldozer had moved, and I figured the construction company must have had an extra set of keys. But that didn't relieve the tremendous guilt I felt.

My relationship with Paul changed after that. I had lost his respect. It wasn't long until his dad was transferred and Paul moved away. But long after he was gone, I continued to think about my heart.

What had caused me to do something so wrong, so careless, and so selfish? I know if I had really cared about Paul, I wouldn't have done it. And what about the construction worker? Did he get fired because he had carelessly left his keys in the ignition? Is it possible his wife and kids suffered because of my insensitive action?

The pain of my childhood indiscretion would not quickly subside. I was plagued by my lack of love.

Whether it was burying the bulldozer keys in the cornfield or the time I bullied Robbie Kirkpatrick just for the fun of it, or other times more serious—over and over through my life I've been faced with the darkness of my heart. I have made choices that hurt others. I have said words that inflicted deep wounds. I have chosen my own needs over those of others.

I recall lying awake at night contemplating my actions and wondering why I do these things. What is going on inside of me when I so selfishly choose to put me first? And how do I get out of this cycle? Do I need to learn more Bible verses? Do I need to go to church more often? Should I confess my sins to a priest?

Some of this came into focus more recently when I tuned in to a podcast interview.

2
I'M TIRED OF THE MASK

God used Marc Maron to speak to me. This may surprise you if you've heard of Marc Maron. Marc has one of the highest-rated podcasts on the planet, with nearly three million downloads every month. It's called *WTF with Marc Maron*—and if you don't know what "WTF" stands for, wait until no children are around and then ask the first person who walks by. Or ask one of your children—they probably know too.

Marc is an actor, comedian, and producer, and the podcast is an interview-style show in which he goes deep with celebrities, musicians, and comedians about their lives. But it's not a comedy show. It's a raw, uncensored look into who people are, the journey they are on, and the successes and failures that brought them to this point in their careers.

The show is laced with profanity and typically has crass and debased content throughout. Many find it too objectionable to listen to regularly. But like a day in which you can be uniquely tuned in to God because of a cloud formation or a fortune cookie, I felt Him tugging at my heart as I listened.

Marc asks questions and gets people talking about the junk in their lives. Although he claims to be an agnostic, he often turns the conversation to faith and to the aching hole inside people that needs something to fill it. He talks frankly about his divorces, alcoholism, screwups, and experimentation with various illegal substances. His guests are vulnerable with him because he opens himself up to them.

My eyes filled with tears one night as I listened to Marc's interview with Norm Macdonald (a comedian made famous on *Saturday Night Live* in the mid-'90s), as he shared his fear of death and his journey to find faith. He talked about God and Christianity and opened up about his desire to learn and know more. He didn't know where to look or whom to talk to, but he said his search continues.

Along with his guests, Marc talks openly about his fear of death and the unknown. He shares with guests his deep-seated jealousy toward others in his industry. He often admits to getting angry and cussing somebody out, but then later going back to tell the person he is sorry. Because he is so open about his doubts and fears, many of his guests also match his vulnerability with their own.

As I listen, I often think, *How is it that this comedian who doesn't believe in God is more open and authentic about his struggles than I am? Why, as a "Christian," do I feel like I can't divulge my true self, like I'm afraid others will think less of me if I expose the blackness of my heart?*

As a member of Marc Maron's audience, my respect for him has increased because I can actually relate to him. As I listen to him admit the darkest truths about his thoughts and motives, I often wonder if I could do the same. Is it possible Jesus could do something in me if I were as honest about my own struggles as Marc Maron is about his?

It seems like there is an unwritten rule that pastors and church leaders, and even regular church attendees, are required to wear masks. It's as though when you become a Christian, you sign a pledge to be fake and you are issued a mask: *Wear this, and don't ever take it off. The whole thing crumbles if people see you without your mask.*

I'm not allowed to admit that, more than a few times, I have dropped the F-bomb after getting cut off in traffic or after hammering my finger instead of the nail. I'm supposed to hide the fact that sometimes I doubt God or the power of prayer or whether miracles can really happen in today's world. I can't say out loud, without being branded a pervert, that I think women are God's most beautiful creation, better than mountains or flowers or babies or stars. I can't confess that some Bible passages make absolutely no sense to me and seem to require more faith than I have to believe.

To admit any of those things is to admit weakness. And to admit weakness is to minimize the power of Jesus within me. And people look to Christian leaders to have all the answers and none of the doubts. So keep your mouth shut. Share your doubts in private with a therapist. And go on pretending all the answers can be found.

But I can't do it. I know, because I've tried. For years I've tried to follow the rules. And I'm really tired. I'm tired of saying things that sound convincing but make no sense. I'm tired of repeating phrases that look great on a Christian bumper sticker or T-shirt but look shallow to the thinking world. I'm tired of smiling at someone and nodding my head on the outside while on the inside thinking, *That is a huge load of crap.*

I'm tired of not being able to ask certain questions. I'm tired of topics you can't bring up anywhere without getting a stupider-than-stupid answer. . .or being symbolically patted on the head as the subject is subtly changed. I'm tired of praying for someone to be healed, and when they die, everyone says, "God answered our prayer, they received ultimate healing"—when what I was really praying for was that the person wouldn't die.

I'm tired of the game. I'm tired of faking it. I'm tired of the mask.

So here is my confession: I still have lots of questions. The older I get, the less I know. The closer I move toward Jesus, the more questions I have. The more I read my Bible, the fewer things seem black and white. I was sure of a whole lot more when I was eighteen. But now, I just don't know.

I don't know why God sometimes seems to answer prayers and other times appears not to care.

I don't know why the Bible is filled with stories of carnage—with God sometimes commanding the mass killing of women and children.

I don't know why Solomon is known as the wisest man who ever lived yet had hundreds of wives and concubines (yeah, those would be women who served him sexually).

I don't know why people who call themselves Christians and know more than I do about the Bible are sometimes the most unloving and self-absorbed jerks.

I don't know why leaders cite church tradition as a basis for their beliefs, when that same church tradition includes corruption, killing, and unspeakable immorality.

There is a lot I don't know. I guess you could say I'm on a journey. It's a journey of searching and finding. It's a journey of skepticism and clarity. It's a journey of seeking and rejecting. It's a journey of understanding and confusion.

And on the journey, as many things have become muddier, a few things have also become clearer. As the foundations of what I've believed have been shaken, I've also made some discoveries that have given me great freedom. I've had to peel away the trappings of Christianity, but as I've done that I think I'm finding the core of who Jesus is.

The more I peel away the rules and expectations and exhausting obligations, the more I find the love of Jesus. These things don't peel away easily—they're a lot like a price tag you pick off an item in a million tiny pieces. But with every scrap removed, there is exposed a treasure of love that was there the whole time—disguised and hidden by religion.

To really peel away all the trappings, I had to go back to the source. What did Jesus Himself say would really make the difference?

3
TATTOOS & TRADITIONS

I lived near South Bend, Indiana, for thirty years. And it didn't take me long after moving there to learn about the Fighting Irish of Notre Dame. I suppose, like any college town, the community in many ways revolves around the campus. When the team is winning, everyone feels great. When they are losing, everyone is a bit sad.

Lou Holtz was the Notre Dame coach when I began following the football team. I remember the 1993 season, when the Irish knocked off Florida State to become the number-one team in the country. The air in South Bend was electric! The next week, in the last game of the regular season, Boston College was killing my team early in the fourth quarter—up by 21 points. I was listening on the radio in my car as the Irish came back with 7 points, then 14, then 20. They scored 22 consecutive points to take the lead by 1. I was fist-pumping out the window and yelling my head off as I raced home so I could watch the end of the game on TV.

I made it home just in time to watch Notre Dame lose the game when Boston College got the ball close enough for a field goal. And as the ball sailed between the uprights, hopes for a national championship were shattered. It would, in fact, be twenty years before Notre Dame would play in another national championship game.

I still have quite a bit of Notre Dame–branded clothing: shirts and hats and such. And when I travel while wearing some of the gear, someone will inevitably pass me at an airport or in a mall and say, "Go Irish!" It's like we're one big happy family.

It's probably no different with Alabama or Michigan or Florida State. A team becomes known by its logo, its colors, or perhaps by a mascot or a mantra ("Roll Tide!" anyone?).

Teams are also known by their traditions. These develop over decades and grow in importance with each passing season. At Notre Dame, they actually mix 24-karat gold into paint and apply it to the football helmets before each game. Another famous tradition is players slapping the famous "Play Like a Champion Today" sign on their way out of the locker room. Another started more than forty years ago, when Sergeant Tim McCarthy of the Indiana State Police began making a driving safety announcement before the fourth quarter to a dead-silent crowd—always ending it with a cheesy pun to the cheers and laughter from the stadium. A more recent tradition is players linking arms in front of the student section at the end of every home game and singing the Alma Mater.

Even though Notre Dame is "my" team, I realize other programs also have great traditions. At Colorado, they run Ralphie the Buffalo around the field before each half. At Arkansas, they "call the hogs"; at Iowa, they take a moment to wave to the kids atop the nearby children's hospital; and at Texas A&M, they honor the "Twelfth Man."

Traditions are part of the glue that holds a fan base together. They are built on from year to year as a program develops. In fact, any school, organization, or even country that wants to develop and secure a following comes up with traditions, logos, hand signals, flags, or other unifying trade-marks that people can rally around.

It could be argued that Jesus left one of the largest, most successful and enduring organizations behind. He started with twelve, but the numbers grew into the thousands and millions, and continue to multiply to this day.

So what tradition did Jesus leave for this movement He started? How would His disciples be known? He didn't give us a logo. We don't have a handshake. There aren't any colors or brands or mantras. That isn't to say we don't have plenty of identifying images. Church history has given us symbols such as the cross or the *ichthys* (fish), as well as many traditions too numerous to list.

But if you peel away all the stuff that religion and culture have added—what did Jesus say or leave behind to pull us all together?

What should being disciples of Jesus look like? How would we as His followers be known? What distinguishing mark would set us all apart?

And what does it mean to be "marked"? You mark your luggage to make sure no one else takes it. You mark your car with a license plate to prove that it is registered and belongs to you. You mark your school assignment with your name so you get proper credit when it is graded.

Some people choose to be marked with a tattoo. I don't have any tattoos, but 45 million Americans are marked with at least one. And the vast majority (83 percent) have no regrets.[1] I remember the first tattoo I ever saw. I was in second grade in my safe little Christian school. Miss Hart gave me permission to go to the restroom, which was really nice because I couldn't wait. The boys' room was straight across the hall, next to the school entrance. I still remember the cinderblock walls, beige tile floors, and brown metal toilet partitions. It smelled like a restroom, and there was a frosted window at the far end, which was usually slanted open, probably to freshen the air. Yet it only seemed to circulate the odor.

When I walked in, I saw adult feet in the first stall. Probably the principal. *Wait, doesn't he have his own bathroom?* Must be the janitor. No problem, I just had to wee-wee, so I walked over to the way-too-tall-for-second-graders urinal and did my business. I flushed, and as I was putting everything back in its place and zipping up, the feet walked out of the stall toward the door.

At that moment, I looked up from my pants while still fastening my belt. At the same time, the feet turned around—and our eyes locked. I froze. There stood a large, sweaty guy with long hair, a scraggly face, dirt-covered arms, filthy clothes, and massive biceps. And on his right arm, the one closest to me, was a tattoo of a skull. If there'd been anything left, I would have wet my pants. I was terrified.

Our school was adding on some classrooms at the time, and this guy was on the construction crew. I'm pretty sure these were before the days of background checks and security perimeters, because here I was, frozen in my tracks, looking at Mr. Skull Tattoo dude, who was standing between me and the safety of my second-grade teacher. We stood there staring at each other for what was probably only a second or two but felt to me more like five minutes. Then he gave me the biggest, warmest smile ever, held up two fingers shaped in a V, said "Peace, man!" and walked out.

I evidently thought any gesture containing fingers was a sin, because I remember running back and telling my teacher, "Miss Hart! A guy with a skull tattoo in the bathroom just gave me the fingers!" She didn't seem alarmed. In hindsight, it seems like she should have been a little concerned that there was a man with a skull tattoo in the boys' bathroom. But it was a nonevent to her. For me, though, it would be forever etched in my memory.

I remember the first time I saw a girl marked with a tattoo. It was at church. At the exact time as I was standing behind her, attempting to sing and focus on God, she leaned forward to get something off the floor. I looked down and saw a tattoo design smiling at me as her shirt pulled up slightly to reveal the small of her back. As I recall, it was much prettier than the skull tattoo.

One of my closest friends is marked with a tattoo. He spent a couple of years thinking about getting one, looking at designs, talking to friends, interviewing artists, asking his wife...and then he finally made the leap. During his two-year research phase, I offered to pay for his tattoo. I said, "Let me pick the image and the location on your body, and I will pay 100 percent of the cost." I told him he wouldn't be able to see it until it was done. For some reason, he didn't think that was a good idea. I could have saved him a bunch of money.

Tattoos are permanent. They are symbols. They often make statements. I know some are spontaneously chosen during an inebriated state of mind (like the girl who had her boyfriend's name tattooed across her face on the first day they met[2]), but most people spend a great deal of time thinking about the mark they will put on their body. It represents something very important to them.

Another type of mark is a scar. A scar might not be chosen, but every scar has a story. I have several on my head due to mishaps with playgrounds, church nurseries, headboards, and furniture that jumped in my way as I was running about. A woman might have a scar across her abdomen that represents sacrifice and love for her baby. A veteran might have a scar with a story of a battle for his country.

When my youngest son was twelve years old, he fell down

while ice-skating. When he attempted to get up, his face was cut by his brother's blade, and then we spent the next several hours at the emergency clinic. He got stitches and was told the scar on his cheek would go away if he faithfully applied a magic lotion. "No way," he announced. "Chicks love scars!" He wasn't about to miss the opportunity for some attention!

People are marked in many ways. Throughout history, slaves or prisoners were branded with a hot iron to indicate possession. Hindus wear a mark on their forehead to express their religion. In the classic book *The Scarlet Letter*, Hester Prynne is found guilty of adultery and forced to wear a scarlet "A" on her dress as a sign of shame.

Whether it's by a tattoo, scar, brand, or sewn-on piece of material, when you are marked, you are on display. You can try to cover up the mark, but people closest to you will eventually discover it. It can't be hidden forever.

I'm fascinated with the idea of being *marked* because of how and when the word is used in the Bible. It's used not once but twice, on arguably two of the most important days in the life of Jesus.

Curious? Turn the page.

4

THE TIME GOD SPOKE

A fascinating thing happens in the early pages of Matthew, the first book in the Bible's New Testament. Most people breeze right over it when they read the passage. But we must understand its implication.

Here is the scene: As far as we know, God hadn't spoken to any man or woman or pastor or priest for more than four hundred years. Talk about deafening silence! You would probably have begun to think He never existed, that maybe the stories handed down from generation to generation about Moses, Abraham, Daniel, and the prophets were all fabricated.

But then God began sending angels to deliver messages: first to Zechariah to tell him that his elderly wife was going to have a baby and that they were to name him John; then six months later to Mary, telling her she would give birth to Jesus; then right away another angel appeared to Joseph, telling him to believe Mary and support her in her pregnancy; and then an entire choir of angels performed in front of some shepherds, also announcing the birth of Jesus.

But still, it hadn't been God Himself speaking. He'd been sending angels or communicating through dreams all about this baby named Jesus. Well, eventually the baby was born, grew up, became a man—and, as far as we know, no more angels appeared and no more messages came from God until Jesus was thirty years old.

That's when everything changed. And that's when we find out how Jesus had been "marked."

It happened on a day when John, the same guy the angel had announced would be born to Zechariah and Elizabeth, was out in the wilderness preaching. He'd been doing this for years and was attracting a lot of attention. He was telling the crowds that God's kingdom was coming and then baptizing them to symbolize a new life. Matthew tells us that people poured out of the surrounding cities and rural areas to hear and see John in action: "There at the Jordan River those who came to confess their sins were baptized into a changed life" (Matthew 3:6 MSG).

Many thought John could be the Messiah. But John knew that wasn't the case. He knew his purpose was to prepare the way for the Messiah. He was related to Jesus, and he probably had grown up hearing the story retold a hundred times about the angel who came and foretold his own birth and the birth of Jesus. My guess is that Jesus and John played together when they were little. Maybe they hung out as teens and talked about the difference God made in their lives.

But on this particular day, far removed from those childhood memories, John was obedient to his call. He was preaching and baptizing, and hundreds were gathering. When he saw some of the religious leaders joining in and getting baptized, just because it was popular, he exploded in anger: "Brood of snakes! What do you think you're doing slithering down here to the river? Do you think a little water on your snakeskins is going to make any difference?" (Matthew 3:7 MSG).

Strong words. You probably won't find John as an example in *How to Win Friends and Influence People*. But he knew that being baptized wasn't going to change anyone's heart.

The people became confused. They thought baptism was part of the whole saving deal. They asked John, "What are we supposed to do?"

In Luke 3:11–14 (MSG), John answered by giving them examples of what a changed life looks like:

"If you have two coats, give one away." He was describing love in action.

"Do the same with your food." More about love.

To tax men: *"No more extortion—collect only what is required by law."* Unexpected love.

To soldiers: *"No shakedowns, no blackmail—and be content with your rations."* In other words, treat all people, all the time, with love.

There it is. Love is the deal. Love is the message. A changed life is a generous, fair, content, and loving life. That's the difference.

And right at that moment, the person who represented and displayed love more than any other human had before or will after, waded into the river. It was Jesus Christ, second cousin to John, the One John knew was the Messiah.

After a short argument about who should baptize whom, John baptized Jesus.

And that was when God spoke for *the first time in more than four hundred years*. This time He didn't send an angel or speak through a dream or vision. It was public and undeniable, and hundreds were watching and listening. When God speaks for the first time in four hundred years, we'd better pay attention:

> *The moment Jesus came up out of the baptismal waters, the skies opened up and he saw God's Spirit—it looked like a dove—descending and landing on him. And along with the Spirit, a voice: "This is my Son, chosen and marked by my love, delight of my life."*
>
>

Matthew 3:16–17 msg
>

One sentence. It's all we got from the God of the Universe—His first words in centuries, introducing His Son publicly for the first time. He told us the one thing we need to know: Jesus is "marked" by the love of God.

Other theologians have translated it, "This is my beloved Son, with whom I am well pleased." I find beauty in both translations. There is a sense that God has stamped or branded Jesus with His own love.

Jesus isn't marked by a tattoo, by a dot on His forehead, by a certain type of clothing, or by a head wrap. We won't know Him because of a medical procedure or because He is unusually tall or good-looking. He looks like everybody else, maybe even a bit on the unattractive side. But He has been marked by the love of God.

And if that's not enough to convince you, God said the same exact words again, three years later, in the *only other instance* He spoke to humans during Jesus' time on this earth. We know it as the "Transfiguration," the time when Jesus appeared to humans in His heavenly form. Peter, James, and John were with Jesus on a mountain, and God said: "This is my Son, marked by my love, focus of my delight. Listen to him" (Matthew 17:5 msg).

Twice, God said that Jesus was "marked by My love." Why not marked by God's holiness? Why not marked by His transcendence or majesty or wisdom?

What could that mean? God could have said anything. . . or nothing. But He told us that His Son, Jesus, was marked by His love. It can't be a coincidence that these were the only words God spoke during Jesus' time on earth and that He said them twice. It must be significant.

No tattoo. No handshake. No team colors or logos or code words. Just the one thing that marked Jesus Christ and the only thing that would mark His followers—love.

5
FAMOUS LAST WORDS

It could be argued that people's most important words are their last words. When people know they are going to die, they tend to get reflective. They think through the whole of their lives and pass along words of wisdom that sum up what they have learned.

In 2007, Randy Pausch, a professor at Carnegie Mellon University, gave his students a lecture. Randy had pancreatic cancer and only a few months to live, so his talk became known as the "Last Lecture" and instantly became a viral hit on YouTube. Millions tuned in to see what a dying man would say in his final words. Randy said, "We cannot change the cards we are dealt, just how we play the hand"—and it carried huge weight.[3]

When my brother-in-law, Patrick McGoldrick, was diagnosed with ALS (Lou Gehrig's disease) in December 2011, he was told he could have up to five years to live. But the disease progressed quickly, and he died twelve months later. In April 2012, Patrick preached what would be his last message. Nearly two thousand people attended—more than 250 were out-of-state visitors who drove or flew in to hear what Patrick would say in his final sermon.[4] Thousands watched his message online in the weeks following. Every word mattered. These were his last public words.

One thing he said still sticks with me: "There are times in the middle of the night when I can't sleep. I will pray over and over, 'It's not about me; it's about You, God. It's not my plan; it's Yours. It's not my will; it's Yours.'"

Patrick also kept a blog, which he updated in his final year of life (PatricksStory.com). In one of his last entries, he wrote: "Just like Joseph, Job, Daniel, Esther, and many others throughout Scripture who ended up in circumstances that they did not ask for and they surely did not like, I daily must choose to focus on submitting to God's will, crying out for His grace, and pointing to my Savior. After all, my sins are still my worst problem and Christ took care of that."[5]

The words matter because a man of God wrote them. But they carry even more weight because they were among the last words he ever wrote.

Pam Butler, a friend of mine from childhood, was diagnosed with cancer in the fall of 2012 and died on March 3, 2013. She kept a blog and wrote these words just six days before she passed: "God may be seeing this trial as a huge opportunity to bring more people to seek God, giving me an unbelievable opportunity to point more people to Christ and build up treasure in heaven, true riches in Christ. Our desire to have this trial removed from us may be taking away that opportunity to further the Kingdom for God."[6]

Amazing wisdom. These words would carry truth even if they had come from you or me. But they carry unbelievable power and influence because Pam shared them as she wrote through her excruciating pain while dying.

So if dying words are so important, and if Jesus is central to your life, isn't it important to consider what He said in His final gathering with the twelve disciples?

We call it the Last Supper. But, of course, that is because we have the benefit of knowing it would be the final time they gathered. The disciples didn't know that. They probably just called it *dinner*. It was just another day, just another meal. But Jesus knew this would be their last meal together: "Jesus knew that the time had come to leave this world to go to the Father" (John 13:1 MSG).

As they were gathered together around a table, eating and talking, Jesus got up, took off His robe, found a towel, and began washing His friends' feet. He was showing them what it means to love each other.

When John wrote about this night, he put it in context for us:

> *Jesus knew that the Father had put all things under his power, and that he had come from God and was returning to God; so he got up from the meal, took off his outer clothing, and wrapped a towel around his waist.*

> JOHN 13:3 4 NIV

Wait. One. Second.

In the same sentence that says Jesus knew He was the most powerful person on the planet, it also says He got up and started washing the disciples' feet. What the what?

If you are the most powerful person in the world, you don't wash dirty feet. That's just wrong. You command someone else to do it. Or better yet, you snap your fingers, and *poof!* The feet are all clean. Or maybe you don't even think about dirty feet. You are focused on other things, like oh, running the universe or something.

But Jesus was trying to teach His friends something. As He worked His way around the table, washing the feet of each disciple, He got to Peter, who loudly protested (of course, Peter did everything loudly). But Jesus talked him down and continued around the table. Then Jesus got up, and in case the disciples were oblivious to what He had just done, He explained:

> *"If I, the Master and Teacher, washed your feet, you must now wash each other's feet. I've laid down a pattern for you. What I've done, you do. I'm only pointing out the obvious. A servant is not ranked above his master; an employee doesn't give orders to the employer. If you understand what I'm telling you, act like it—and live a blessed life"*
>
> JOHN 13:14–17 MSG

In one of His last actions before His arrest and subsequent death, Jesus gave His disciples an incredibly clear illustration on what it means to serve each other. He was tearing down every social boundary and preconceived notion of power and position and saying, "This is how you love each other."

What followed might be the most powerful words Jesus ever spoke. Remember, these are final words from a man who would soon be condemned to death. The disciples didn't know it—but Jesus did. So, He chose His words carefully as He summed up everything He had taught them for the past three years. This was it. These were His final words. These were the words that carry the most weight because they were among His last:

> *"A new command I give you: Love one another. As I have loved you, so you must love one another. By this everyone will know that you are my disciples, if you love one another."*
>
> JOHN 13:34–35 NIV

Just thirty-five words. And yet He said the same thing three times in a row.

Love one another. Love one another. Love one another.

It all comes down to love.

If Jesus had been long-winded (like many preachers I know), He might have said it this way: "You won't be known by any secret handshakes. We aren't going to build churches that all have the same label on the side of the building. There won't be any logos or branding or websites or products. There is only one thing that will set us apart. There is only one way people will know you are My disciples—by your love for each other. Love well, and it will change the world."

And if anyone in the room was confused by what it meant to "love one another," he only had to think back a few minutes to when Jesus was on His knees washing the dirt off their feet.

This. Changes. Everything.

What if I ignored all the expectations and rules of Christianity and focused on the one thing Jesus said would define His disciples? What if love became the filter through which everything I did or said flowed?

Instead of the popular "What Would Jesus Do?" maybe the right question is "How Would Jesus Love?"

- How would Jesus love others in a political discussion?

- How would Jesus love someone who is contemplating an abortion?

- How would Jesus love a friend going through a divorce?

- How would Jesus love the person who cut me off in traffic?

- How would Jesus love the family who just lost a parent?

- How would Jesus love the guy who just got my unmarried daughter pregnant?

- How would Jesus love my boss, who treats me like a slave?

- How would Jesus love your daughter when she comes out as transgender?

- How would Jesus love the neighbor who just sued me over a property line dispute?

- How would Jesus love my relative who borrowed a lot of money from me and never paid it back?

- How would Jesus love my gay friend who invited me to his wedding?

- How would Jesus love the family you think may have crossed the border illegally and are living off government welfare?

- How would Jesus love the homeless guy begging on the curb?

If love becomes the one filter through which I process every decision, every action, and every word, then it seems impossible that my life wouldn't change. If I were marked by love—as visible as a tattoo or a burn on my face—wouldn't that make a difference?

It sounds a little cliché, but isn't it all about love? I'm not talking about a let's-all-sit-in-a-circle-and-touch-toes type of love. This isn't about wet kisses or sappy greeting cards. It's not a pie-in-the-sky love that has no basis in reality.

Jesus was talking about a world-changing, lay-your-life-down-for-your-friend type of love. It's the type of love that made it easy for Him to wash His friends' dirty, stinky feet. It's the type of love that enabled Him to not react when He was beaten and mocked. It's the type of love that gave Him the ability to forgive those who were killing Him and mocking His Father.

This is as real as it gets.

6
I DON'T WANT TO BE CALLED
A CHRISTIAN

It's been a journey trying to figure out what I am.

I'm definitely no longer a fundamentalist. I grew up on a steady diet of sermon recordings by Curtis Hutson, Jerry Falwell, and John R. Rice. They all claimed to hold to the fundamentals of the Bible and preached strongly against "heretics" who taught otherwise. Churches would use the "fundamentalist" label on their street signs, which was a secret signal to the faithful that "we are right" and others are not. Oh, if it were all so black and white.

Then I became an evangelical, which was kind of like a grace-filled version of a conservative Christian. That worked for a while, until the "evangelical" took the place of the "fundamentalist" and became known more for what they stood *against* than what they stood *for*. In a poll sponsored by Gallup, David Kinnaman and Gabe Lyons found that most people view evangelical Christians as hypocritical, too focused on getting converts, homophobic, sheltered, too political, and judgmental.[7] And why would I want to be branded as such?

In high school I worked as a volunteer for the Ronald Reagan campaign of 1984 and became a vocal member of the Moral Majority. In those days, it was popular to be conservative, Republican, evangelical, and Christian. In fact, in many ways, those terms were all used interchangeably. Today? I think those terms hurt more than they help.

In some ways, I'm a political conservative. But when I hear the vitriolic, hateful fighting on TV, I want to stay as far away from the "conservative" label as possible.

In other ways, I'm a liberal. But if you believe what you hear in some circles, liberals are all going to hell because they hate families and America and Israel—so I don't want that label either.

I used to be a Baptist. But do I want to put myself in the same category as the folks from Westboro Baptist Church, who picket in front of military funerals, holding signs saying "God hates fags"? I don't think so.

For twenty years I was a pastor at a United Methodist church. The inner-circle joke was that you could say anything about a Methodist and you'd be right. Because some stand for nothing and some stand for everything. It's no longer a label that means anything.

But you know what? I don't want to be called a conservative or a liberal. I don't want to be known as a Baptist or a Methodist. And I don't want to spend any energy explaining to someone whether I'm a Calvinist or an Arminian.

In fact, let me be brutally honest. *Most days I don't even want to be called a Christian.*

I'm dead serious. So much evil has been done through the centuries in the name of Christianity. Maybe we just need to leave the term behind and start over. It has too much baggage. Whether it was the Crusades or Medieval Inquisition of yesteryear, or the pedophile priest scandals of the current era, Christianity has gotten a bad name.

A few years ago, a Christian pastor in Florida publicly

burned a Koran to incite Muslims across the world. A group of Christians from Kansas—the aforementioned Westboro Baptist Church—travels around the country trying to get attention with signs like "Planes Crash, God Laughs" and "Pray for More Dead Soldiers."

I read in the news about a St. Louis pastor who ate a meal at Applebee's, and instead of leaving a tip, he wrote on the receipt, "I give God 10%. Why should you get 18%?"[8] Everywhere you turn, you hear of another "Christian" who is giving Jesus a bad name.

Susan K. Smith said it this way:

> I hate it when I hear someone say, "I am a Christian." Immediately, I recoil, because most times when people say that phrase, it is said with a sense of arrogance and superiority. When I hear those four words, I think not of kindness and love, but of bullying, judgmentalism, exclusivity, unforgiveness, cruelty and hypocrisy.[9]

Read that again. If you grew up going to church and trying to do the right thing, that should make you very sad.

That's why I don't want to be called a Christian. Calling myself a Christian associates me with people with whom I don't want to be associated. It forces on me a filter I can't control. As soon as I say I'm a Christian, people put me in a category based on their understanding of what a Christian is—and that understanding is often colored by their personal experiences, good or bad. And many (maybe most?) people believe there is more bad than good. I don't want to chance that.

The word *Christian* (or *Christianos* in Greek) was originally a Roman term of derision for those who followed Jesus Christ.

They were mocking these early believers with that word. Similarly, in the lead-up to the 2008 election, people who were rabid followers of Hillary Clinton were sometimes called *Clintonistas* and those who held undying loyalty to Barack Obama were labeled *Obamaniacs*. These were not terms of endearment but labels meant to categorize and ridicule. In 2016, those who supported Trump received the label *deplorables*, a term meant to demean but that Trump's followers wore like a badge of honor, sometimes on their T-shirts.

The only known time one of the early disciples used the term *Christian* was when Peter encouraged believers not to be ashamed when they suffer (again lending credibility to the idea that, even within the church the term was mockery). It actually meant something in the first century. It was used specifically to denote a follower of Jesus. They were one and the same.

Not anymore. In today's world, at least in America, the word is either filled with baggage because of the actions or inactions of professing Christians through the ages. Or, it means absolutely nothing. For some, calling yourself a Christian has little to do with Jesus and a great deal to do with culture. Wearing the term is as easy and acceptable as putting on your Calvin Kleins or grabbing your iPhone.

I once typed "Christians are" into a Google search field and these were the first five search results:

- Christians are annoying.
- Christians are hate-filled.
- Christians are hypocritical.
- Christians are delusional.
- Christians are narrow-minded.

In Bing, you'll see the words *stupid* and *crazy* in the top results.

Don't get me wrong: I don't have a problem with Jesus. My problem is with Christianity. I think too many people have made Christianity their religion and the Bible their idol. Rather than following the steps and words of Jesus, they have bowed to a cultural definition of Christianity. They think going to church and hanging with other Christians is the thing that separates them from culture and gets them a good standing with Jesus. They think studying the Bible will bring the eternal life they want, but they miss Jesus in the meantime.

That's why I don't want to be known as a conservative.

Why I don't want to be known as a Methodist.

Why I don't even want to be known as a Christian.

In fact, if someone is going to label me, I want to be known as a follower of Jesus. The Bible term for that is *disciple*.

We don't use the word *disciple* much in today's world. Just like the word *follower*, it requires further definition. No one is just a follower. They are a follower of someone or something. Likewise, no one is just a disciple. They are a disciple of someone.

Every few years, a major cult leader makes it into the headlines and you hear about his or her followers. David Koresh led the disciples of the Branch Davidian sect to their deaths in Waco, Texas. Jim Jones led disciples who followed him to their deaths in 1978, taking three hundred children with them. Although these are terrible incidents, they are indicative of what a disciple is. A disciple believes so fully in whom they are following that they are willing to die for that person.

Although less commonly used in the context, I've heard the term *disciple* in the management world. I've read articles about a CEO who is described as a "disciple of Jim Collins" or a "disciple of Peter Drucker." It indicates they follow and agree with just about everything that leader says.

The focus isn't on the follower. It is on *who* they are following. The early disciples were known as Christians because they were followers of Christ.

I think it's too late to try to redefine the word *Christian* for our world. That ship has already sailed. It isn't my passion or interest to turn the strong tide of our culture away from what they think of Christianity. Rather than change people's language, I want them to see Jesus in me. I want to live in such a way that my neighbors will remark, "There is something different about you." I want to respond to conflict the way Jesus would respond. I want to treat my wife and kids the way Jesus would treat them. I want to run my business affairs with the highest integrity—no cut corners, no white lies, no manipulation tactics.

I want to be different. I want to be marked by love. If people follow me, I want to lead them to Jesus.

But what does that even mean? What is a "disciple" of Jesus? What would it take to show this world a different type of Christian? Is it really all about love? What about holiness?

So many questions. This is going to mean adopting an entirely different way of thinking—a way of thinking I started learning from Darrell many years ago.

7
LESSONS IN A
WHITE PICKUP TRUCK

Darrell was a round man and not very tall. He breathed loudly and drove a big white pickup truck. Darrell didn't really fit in at the independent Baptist church my family attended because he asked way too many questions. But he loved helping people, and he especially loved kids.

As a middle school kid, I started volunteering for the church bus ministry with Darrell. Every Sunday we would get in bus number 2 and Dave Turner would drive us into the inner city of Des Moines to pick up kids and take them to Sunday school. We'd cram the bus full of sixty or seventy kids, sing songs and play games all the way to church, then repeat the gig as we took all the kids home after Sunday school.

And each Saturday morning I would hop in the passenger seat of Darrell's big white truck, and we would visit every family of every kid on our route. We would ask how they were doing, see if we could pray for them, and remind them to be ready for the bus the next morning.

Between visits, as I was riding alongside Darrell in his big white truck, he would ask me questions that would mess with my faith. Darrell owned a nursing home and told me he could get me a job in the kitchen if I wanted it. I told him I wouldn't work on Sundays. Why? Because it's a sin, of course. Sunday is a day of rest. (It's amazing how much I knew as a fourteen-year-old.)

He said, "Really? So we should just let all the people in hospitals and nursing homes fend for themselves on Sunday?"

I didn't have a good answer for that.

He asked me who should administer the medicine and bury the dead? Should we also tell all the police and fire departments we don't want their officers and firefighters working on Sunday?

Hmm. Can we talk about something else?

Another time we had a big debate about rock music. I had recently taken an entire week out of school to attend the Bill Gothard Institute in Basic Life Principles seminar. My pastors agreed with Gothard's teaching that if you were a fan of rock music, you could not have victory in your moral life. Rock music is sensual, they held, and you can't combine the sensual with the spiritual. We even had a high school bonfire during a "revival" crusade when we brought in our albums and smutty books and watched them burn. I didn't have any rock albums, only a few upbeat Christian titles from artists like Don Francisco and the Imperials. But since, I was told, you can't have "Christian rock" any more than you can have "Christian pornography," my albums needed to burn too. Yay, Jesus.

Darrell asked me why rock music was bad. Was it the beat? The singers? The people playing the music? The lyrics? The tempo?

I didn't know the answer. I just knew that every spiritual leader in my life told me it was wrong. And I couldn't point to one person who listened to rock music I wanted to emulate (an indication of the bubble I lived in).

We argued back and forth, and he poked holes in all the things I believed but had never really thought about. We talked about when Jesus would return, how to determine the will of God, whether there would be animals in heaven, when the earth was created, and even dispensational theology (a belief system I followed for years that helped me make sense of everything in the Bible I couldn't otherwise explain).

I don't think I agreed with anything Darrell said at the time. There were days I just wanted him to stop talking. I already knew what Christianity was—a list of things *not* to do (don't dance, go to movies, or go swimming when there are girls in the pool) and other things *to* do (read the Bible every day and obey your parents). I knew that only churches with "Fundamentalist, Bible-believing, Independent" written on their signs were right and all other churches taught the feel-good social gospel. I knew that all television evangelists were false prophets, especially ones like Billy Graham, who used the "easy Gospel" to save thousands at one time.

But Darrell was different. He didn't tell me what to believe. He taught me how to think. He encouraged me to actually look in my Bible and see what it had to say about issues rather than just believe what I had been taught.

A few years later, I graduated high school and joined a small religious organization that hosted revival meetings and multimedia productions in churches across the United States. I left the safe, protective haven of Pleasant Hill, Iowa, but began working with an organization that held most of the same beliefs and standards as my parents and my church. However, I would soon be exposed to faith-stretching situations that would challenge my beliefs to their very core.

In my first year on the road, we performed at 250 locations. That meant I saw 250 different churches—Baptist, Presbyterian, Methodist, Pentecostal, and a bunch of no-name churches.

And you know what I found? At every church there were people who loved Jesus, who wanted to live lives that pleased God, and who were trying to take their next step toward Christ. *Wait, this isn't possible. These churches are supposed to be teaching apostasy, and their leaders should be more interested in money than faith.*

In that initial year, I also stayed in 250 different homes and listened to 250 different host "parents" tell me how they met Jesus and why their faith mattered to them. I heard stories of radical life change. I stayed with families who were divorced yet still accepted at their churches. And I talked with parents who were trying to hang on as they had just learned of their teen's drug dependency or pregnancy. I lost count of the number of people who told me they were first introduced to Jesus at a Billy Graham crusade. *What? I thought he was a heretic!*

At one stop in Boca Raton, Florida, we had a day off in the same town where a contemporary Christian singer was hosting a concert. We took a team vote on whether to go to the concert. I voted against it (remember, rock music was a sin), but majority ruled, so we went to the concert.

I can't explain my emotions that night. I think I can only explain that night by saying *I met God.* I'm not talking about a shallow experience manipulated by an entertainer. I felt the presence of God like never before. And honestly, it was confusing to me. There were drums and electric guitars, and the singers actually moved around (a.k.a. *danced*) on the stage— all things I had thought were evil. But it was so God-focused. *How is this possible?*

After the concert, a few of us who had grown up the same way talked late into the evening about what we had just experienced. It was like our souls had been revived, yet it was from a source we thought was *supposed* to be godless.

Underneath it all, I think I wondered if I had been duped

growing up. If my leaders had told me that certain kinds of music were evil, yet my experience was telling me exactly the opposite, then what other lies had they told me? And what were they trying to protect?

I started to see holes in what I had been taught, so I began to question *everything*. It's like I had to disassemble every single "truth" I had ever learned so I could then reassemble my faith on something solid. What was I going to believe?

I don't think anyone duped me on purpose. They truly believed what they had told me. No one had started each day asking, "How many people can I deceive today?" It was much subtler than that.

But it's been thirty years since that experience, and I think, to some degree, I am still untangling and reassembling. Every month or so, I become aware of another evidence of the vines of legalism that for so long have been intertwined throughout every part of my soul. It's amazing how deep it goes. And it is amazing how liberating it is to become disentangled—and to rediscover the essence of the life to which Jesus calls us.

Legalism puts holiness (i.e. following the rules) and love up against each other as competitors. You must choose. And so entire generations of Christians grow up going to church and following the rules. But they are sometimes the most unloving and ungrateful humans around.

I began thinking about this more deeply after an encounter with a man named Bob.

8
BOB'S SIMPLE QUESTION

My youth pastor was a Bishop. Not like a Catholic or Methodist bishop. His name was Greg Bishop. We called him "Pastor Bishop." It's kind of like calling me a "man guy" or saying you are going to drive your "auto car." We thought his name was kind of funny.

Pastor Bishop just knew I was going to be a pastor, much earlier than even I did. Maybe he saw some potential or skill in me, or perhaps he just thought I'd never be able to do anything else.

In our denomination (which really wasn't a denomination, but more of an association of churches), a pastor would become a pastor by studying for weeks and then answering questions and defending his beliefs at a grueling interview that would last for up to eight hours.

As he worked at preparing me for ministry, Pastor Bishop would take me around central Iowa, where we attended ordination councils. I remember sitting in small auditoriums watching the candidate seated all alone behind a table on the stage while a group of about twenty older (and presumably wiser) pastors peppered him with theological questions, one after another.

They would talk about predestination, inerrancy, irresistible grace, and a hundred other topics with lots of big words and nuanced definitions. I remember thinking, *I'm pretty sure I would flunk this quiz.*

I went to a few of these, and I remember one question from a pastor who was probably nearing eighty years old. He went to all the ordinations, but as I recall, he only asked one question. And it was the same question each time: "Which attribute of God is most dominant—His holiness or His love?"

I guess I remember that question so well because of the ensuing conversation I overheard during the lunch break. Another pastor asked, "Bob, why do you ask that question at every single ordination? And, if you are so curious about the question, how come you never seem to care which way it is answered?"

"I don't have any idea what the correct answer is," Bob replied. "I just want to make sure every young pastor is struggling with the question."

Hmm, interesting reply. And a question I've been chewing on in the nearly forty years since. I'm becoming more convinced that there is a right answer—and it's right in front of us. Consider the interaction Jesus had with some really smart religious leaders in Matthew 22.

Here is the context: Jesus had gone through an eventful few days. First, He was ushered into Jerusalem on a donkey with the crowd cheering "Hosanna!" From there, He went straight to the temple, where we find Him angrily overturning tables and kicking out merchants who were grossly overcharging for sacrifices. All the while, people sang His praises while the religious leaders were getting pretty ticked. (Imagine how you'd react if someone walked into your house and overturned all your furniture and then walked out.)

The next day, Jesus was tired and hungry (today we call that *hangry*) and found a fig tree with no figs. So what did He do? He cursed it to death. This is not hyperbole. It literally died on the spot.

Then He headed back to the temple to teach some more—and this really made the religious leaders mad. They started questioning Him: "Show us your credentials. Who authorized you to teach here?" (Matthew 21:23 msg). Jesus wouldn't answer them. He wouldn't be sucked into their tricks. Instead, He turned it right around and asked *them* a question. They decided it was too risky to answer with the crowd that was watching, so they decided not to respond to His question and instead found a place at the edge of the crowd.

Then Jesus started telling stories. He talked about a farmer with two sons who each responded differently to their father. He talked about the greedy farmhands who were supposed to be caring for their masters' farm but instead acted as though they owned it. The tension was building as Jesus continued teaching. Everyone listening knew the stories were about the leaders in the back of the room:

> When the chief priests and the Pharisees heard Jesus' parables, they knew he was talking about them. They looked for a way to arrest him, but they were afraid of the crowd because the people held that he was a prophet.
> MATTHEW 21:45–46 NIV

Jesus told one more story before the religious leaders couldn't stand it anymore. They came from the back of the room with a plan to trick Jesus: "That's when the Pharisees plotted a way to trap him into saying something damaging" (Matthew 22:15 msg).

Once again, their trick didn't work. Jesus again spun it around on them and made them answer a question. They came at Him again. He was getting a bit frustrated with their continued attacks. Before He answered, He said: "You're off base on two counts: You don't know your Bibles, and you don't know how God works" (Mathew 22:29 MSG).

Do you see what's happening here? Jesus had been teaching all day, and between every story these spiritual leaders walked up and pestered Him like swarming mosquitoes on a hot summer day. He swatted them away by turning their questions around on them. But they kept coming back. He never answered directly. It was always a redirect.

Until what happened next.

Suddenly, with one question, everything changed.

In one more effort to trick Jesus, they asked a loaded question: "Teacher, which is the greatest commandment in the Law?" (Matthew 22:36 NIV).

Yep, that's loaded. They just asked Him to pick which one of the 613 laws was the most important. This was a political hot potato being asked by the leaders whose job it was to hold people to *all* the commandments.

Would He say "Don't oppress the weak" is the greatest commandment?

Or perhaps "Don't take revenge on others"?

Maybe He would say the greatest commandment is to not worship idols. Or perhaps don't do magic. Or honor your parents. Or don't steal.

Would He say "Rest on the Sabbath" is the most important law?

None of those. Jesus didn't blink. He didn't hesitate, and He didn't redirect or refuse to answer their question. He jumped in with both feet and answered boldly:

> " *'Love the Lord your God with all your passion and*
> *prayer and intelligence.' This is the most important,*
> *the first on any list. But there is a second to set*
> *alongside it: 'Love others as well as you love yourself.'*
> *These two commands are pegs; everything in God's*

Law and the Prophets hangs from them."

MATTHEW 22:37–40 MSG

Whoa! This was huge. It was almost heretical. In effect, Jesus was saying, "All of Scripture is *not* equally important. In fact, there are two things more important than anything else. And everything revolves around these two commands."

Love.

That's it, pure and simple.

Love God. Love others. Get these two right, and everything else will come together. Get these wrong, and you'll never be able to make sense of life.

Are you beginning to notice a trend?

First, the only known words God the Father spoke about Jesus while He was on earth (and it happened twice) was that Jesus was "marked by My love."

Second, in His final words to His disciples, Jesus told them to love each other. In fact, He said His disciples will be known by their love for one another.

And in this story, when the religious leaders asked Jesus about the most important commandment in the Bible, without hesitation He said we are to "love God and love others."

This isn't accidental. There is something going on here we might miss. Why, when we are to be marked by God's love, are we instead known as being judgmental? Why, when we are to be known by the way we love each other, are we instead known as being political and hypocritical? If the most important commandment is to love God and love others, yet we sue each other, divorce our spouses, and abandon our families at the same rate as those who don't claim to follow Jesus,[10] then how can we expect anyone to want what we have?

Love is the difference maker. It changes everything.

Most of all, it changes our hearts.

9
THE CHANNELS BETWEEN
THE CHANNELS

Cable television was a new phenomenon when I was a kid, and we were early adopters. We had one of those remote controls that was the size of a book, had thirteen levers, and was connected by a cord stretched around the room to the back of the TV. Even better, it clunked every time you changed channels. But it was cool because we didn't have to walk across the room anymore.

It didn't take long for me to figure out that you could hold the levers in just the right way to get the channels between the channels—you know, the ones we weren't supposed to get. They were fuzzy, but I saw things I had never seen before. I saw women. Beautiful women. It was like a blind man gaining sight and viewing a sunset for the first time. Oh my!

One time when I was enjoying the channels between the channels, my mom walked into the room. She was disgusted. I tried to pretend I was just changing channels and the remote got stuck. But she knew I was lying. And I knew she knew I was lying. I maintained my story but could feel her deep disappointment. I felt dirty.

I guess it was guilt. I had done something wrong. By the

look in my mom's eyes, I knew I had crossed a line. But, honestly, I didn't know *why* it was wrong. I couldn't understand why something that felt so right could be wrong. It didn't make sense that God would create me with a drive and hunger for sexual satisfaction and then put it on a list of big bad sins.

And, as everyone knew, sexual sins were the worst.

A good friend of mine, Patty, was suddenly gone from school one day with rumors flying around that she was pregnant. It was like crossing sexual lines was worthy of banishment. And sins like gossip or slander or anger or bitterness? Totally acceptable—they were in the "just try harder" category.

That is especially difficult for a teenage boy dealing with sexual urges that feel overpowering at times. Sometimes my sex drive seemed like a skyscraper, and I was the little boy standing next to it looking up with my eyes wide open. I was so small and it was so big, and I didn't stand a chance.

When I was about twelve years old, I got a paper route, and I delivered papers seven days a week. I could reach into my bag, grab a paper, fold and wrap it with a rubber band, and toss it from the street onto a porch with deadly accuracy—all in about two seconds. . .and while riding my bike. Yeah, I was *that* kid.

My route included five large apartment buildings, each with three floors. One day I discovered someone had left some pornographic magazines in the laundry room at the end of the hallway.

It took me longer to finish my paper route that day.

I was pretty sure I was the only kid who struggled with these urges. Looking back, I know that's ridiculous, but at the time I just knew it had to be true. No one else had the same evil thoughts or desires I did. And if they did, there was no way their thoughts were as evil or desires as impure as mine.

I felt helpless. Praying never helped, and neither did lists of do's and don'ts. Promises to God to never mess up again didn't do me any good either. And until I was twenty years old, I never knew anyone else who had the same struggle. Everyone else was a saint, and I was a closet pervert.

It's a bit of a mystery, because I know God is holy. I know I'm supposed to flee immorality and not look at women lustfully. But those truths, which had been drilled into me from my earliest days, never helped me in my battle with temptation for long. As a teen and young adult, I lived in the endless cycle of victory, temptation, sin, despair, conviction, forgiveness—and back to victory. Except it seemed like I spent more time on the "sin" side of the cycle than on the "victory" side.

When I lived in Indiana, I heard my pastor, Mark Beeson, use the illustration of the three hats of Satan. He taught that Satan uses three different tactics on us. (Mark put on three different hats to illustrate.) In my endless cycle of failure and victory, I could see the devil putting on the three hats as he worked against me:

Tempter—Satan finds a way to tempt me. Perhaps it is a subtle image that triggers a curious search, followed by a mouse click or phone tap.

Promoter—Like a whisper in my ear, Satan tells how great things will be if I go down this path. The feelings of respect and honor will be coupled with a deep satisfaction. Nothing could be better.

Accuser—After I fail, Satan is right there to tell me what a despicable human being I am, how no one is as bad as I am, and that God could never forgive someone who did something so abhorrent.

Even though I know what is right, and I can see exactly

what Satan is trying to do to mess me up, I still don't have the power in the moment to divert my plans and choose the right path. I just can't do it.

I think the apostle Paul felt the same way when he wrote:

> What I don't understand about myself is that I decide one way, but then I act another, doing things I absolutely despise. So if I can't be trusted to figure out what is best for myself and then do it, it becomes obvious that God's command is necessary.
>
> But I need something more! For if I know the law but still can't keep it, and if the power of sin within me keeps sabotaging my best intentions, I obviously need help! I realize that I don't have what it takes. I can will it, but I can't do it. I decide to do good, but I don't really do it; I decide not to do bad, but then I do it anyway. My decisions, such as they are, don't result in actions. Something has gone wrong deep within me and gets the better of me every time.
>
> Romans 7:15–20 MSG

Part of you probably wants to say "amen!" But another part may be saying, "Oh my! That's me." There are times we are all aware of the darkness in our own hearts. Let's face it: Sometimes we do the right thing, and other times we don't even want to.

Let's consider this another way. . . .

10
A 200-POUND BAG OF SEWAGE

I'm guessing you can identify with me. We each carry around the weight of knowing our own junk, along with the overwhelming sense that we must be the only one. There comes a time when that weight becomes unbearable.

You know there is something deeply wrong inside of you, and you also know there is nothing you can do to fix it. It's like you are carrying around a 200-pound bag of sewage on your shoulders. No one can see it, but it is there. Even when people get a glimpse of the weight you carry, they don't know what's in the bag. But you know. And it's ugly.

The Old Testament prophet Jeremiah said it this way: "The heart is hopelessly dark and deceitful, a puzzle that no one can figure out" (Jeremiah 17:9 MSG).

People try all kinds of things in an effort to remove the weight of their own bag of sewage and ease their own pain and sense of emptiness.

Perhaps you've tried alcohol or tobacco or drugs to make the pain of your own condition go away. And it may have worked for a while. You laugh and have fun and feel good. . . for a few hours. But then the sorrow and self-judgment and excruciating guilt return, heavier than they were before. So, you return again and again to your substance of choice. But it is a downward cycle that leads to the death of your soul.

Or maybe you've tried to fill the void with sex. There is nothing like being skin-to-skin with someone you know totally accepts you, wants you, and admires you. The pursuit is a challenge, and the act is pure ecstasy. But you wake up beside that person and realize it is all based on pretense—you are using her to feel better about yourself, and she's using you for the same. But you return to this drug again and again because it feels good. And if you can feel good even for a few minutes, you'll take it because it's better than the aching nothingness in your soul.

Some live as though money is the solution—as though the pain in their souls can be neutralized by a car or vacation or new pair of jeans. Leonardo DiCaprio plays the part of Jordan Belfort in *The Wolf of Wall Street*, a movie based on the true story about a guy who had it all but wanted more. Even Hollywood got it right in the movie's tagline: "More is never enough."

Our own worlds may not be filled with yachts and million-dollar vacations, but we know the futility of trying to quiet the noise in our souls or fix the brokenness of our hearts by spending more money. And so, our houses are filled with remnants of products that once held the hope of wholeness but now are just daily reminders of how empty our lives really are.

We aren't alone in our condition, as Paul points out:

> *Basically, all of us, whether insiders or outsiders, start out in identical conditions, which is to say that we all start out as sinners. Scripture leaves no doubt about it: "There's nobody living right, not even one, nobody who knows the score, nobody alert*

for God. They've all taken the wrong turn; they've all wandered down blind alleys. No one's living right; I can't find a single one."

ROMANS 3:9–12 MSG

That is supposed to make us feel good, but it only adds to the hopeless feeling that comes with the realization that there is nothing we can do about our condition. *I am broken*, we think, *and there is not a thing I can do about it.*

Some don't choose drugs or sex or money to fill the void; many choose religion or religious activity. There is a sense that if we do enough good, it will balance the ledger and offset our bad thoughts or actions. So we go to church every week and help out at the food kitchen or volunteer at the hospital. We like helping people, but at the end of the day it just feels like more activity that doesn't do anything about the real pain.

Sometimes the guilt we carry causes us to skip church for weeks at a time because we are convinced we don't measure up to *those* people. *They are better than me*, we think. *If they knew the real me, I wouldn't even be allowed to come.*

It doesn't seem to matter what we do, the pain won't go away. The feeling of having no purpose and no reason to be on this planet is ever present. The gnawing ache in our hearts can't even be adequately explained, but it is there.

And the real problem? There is absolutely nothing we can do to fix ourselves. Many have tried everything I've listed and more, but they find that trying to fix themselves is a hopeless endeavor.

What I'm about to say might seem trite or cliché. It might seem utterly ridiculous in light of movies you've seen or bumper stickers you've mocked or people you've known who have said the same thing.

But the fact is this: You have to stop trying. You have to give up. The answer isn't found in an activity or church service. There is nothing you can *do* to make yourself better. The only answer is in a person. The only answer is Jesus.

You might be saying to yourself, "Whatever! I've tried Jesus." Perhaps you've tried *religion*. Perhaps you've put your faith in a person who claimed to represent Jesus. Perhaps you've been manipulated by one of the many lies embedded in church history. I get that. It is so easy to reject Jesus because of those who purport to be His messengers. We've all seen the intolerance or hate or judgment that has come from the "church," and we want to reject it all. Throw out baby Jesus with the bathwater!

We've watched power and prestige go to the head of a pastor or priest or televangelist, and it has turned our stomachs. Jesus said it this way:

> *"You've observed how godless rulers throw their weight around," he said, "and when people get a little power how quickly it goes to their heads. It's not going to be that way with you. Whoever wants to be great must become a servant. Whoever wants to be first among you must be your slave. That is what the Son of Man has done: He came to serve, not to be served—and then to give away his life in exchange for many who are held hostage."*
>
> MARK 10:42–45 MSG

How many have rejected Jesus because of one of these godless rulers or power-hungry leaders? But that isn't the Jesus way.

Jesus is love. He came as a servant. He came to give His life for you. Not because you've done everything right, but because He could see past your junk.

Your only solution is to lay down your shame at Jesus' feet and let Him take care of it. You have to stop trying, stop struggling, stop doing more or doing better. You have to let it all go.

Paul says we are "utterly incapable" of living right:

> *Since we've compiled this long and sorry record as sinners. . .and proved that we are utterly incapable of living the glorious lives God wills for us, God did it for us. Out of sheer generosity he put us in right standing with himself. A pure gift. He got us out of the mess we're in and restored us to where he always wanted us to be. And he did it by means of Jesus Christ.*
>
> ROMANS 3:22–24 MSG

It's not about anything you can do or fix or manufacture. God did it for you. He takes away your shame and puts you in right standing with Himself. *A pure gift.*

I heard a guy illustrate this truth by stretching a long string across a room. At the left end, he wrote the names of Adolf Hitler and Osama bin Laden. At the right end, he wrote "Jesus." Then he threw out some famous names and asked the audience where he should write them down. People like Joseph Stalin and the cowards who recently killed civilians in a Manchester concert, in an Orlando nightclub, and at a Las Vegas country music festival were written toward the left end (pretty close to Hitler). And names like Billy Graham, Mother Teresa, and Mahatma Gandhi were written about 80 percent to the right—not next to Jesus, but close.

Then he asked us to consider where our own names would go on this string that represented pure evil at one extreme and sinlessness at the other. Most everyone in the room admitted to putting their name somewhere in the middle. I think it made some of us feel pretty good—we weren't as bad as a murdering psychopath. But I also think it also made some feel pretty humbled to even be in the same universe as some of the greatest saints of our time.

He then asked us to consider this verse: "For everyone has sinned; we all fall short of God's glorious standard" (Romans 3:23 NLT).

He explained that no one—not Billy Graham or even your grandmother—is good enough on his or her own to measure up to God's standards. No one can do it, so God had to make a way.

His plan was Jesus. In the most selfless act of all time, Jesus lived on earth, experienced pain and mockery and temptation, and then died to express His love for you and me. When we understand the expression of love Jesus showed us on the cross, then our bag of sewage begins to get lighter. Jesus' invitation is clear:

> *"Are you tired? Worn out? Burned out on religion? Come to me. Get away with me and you'll recover your life. I'll show you how to take a real rest. Walk with me and work with me—watch how I do it. Learn the unforced rhythms of grace. I won't lay anything heavy or ill-fitting on you. Keep company with me and you'll learn to live freely and lightly."*
> MATTHEW 11:28–30 MSG

And isn't that what we want? To live freely and lightly, to live without the burden of carrying our own sewage.

Jesus did it for us:

Christ arrives right on time to make this happen.
He didn't, and doesn't, wait for us to get ready. He
presented himself for this sacrificial death when we
were far too weak and rebellious to do anything
to get ourselves ready. And even if we hadn't been
so weak, we wouldn't have known what to do
anyway. We can understand someone dying for a
person worth dying for, and we can understand
how someone good and noble could inspire us to
selfless sacrifice. But God put his love on the line for
us by offering his Son in sacrificial death while we
were of no use whatever to him.

ROMANS 5:6–8 MSG

Our only hope is Jesus. When we give our lives to Him, we are forever marked by His love.

11
JESUS AS JEWELRY

I recently read a poem that attempts to describe what happens to you after you meet Jesus. Here is part of it (along with my commentary):

Since I Met You. . .

More lovely is the sound
Of the birds in song,
Since I met You,
Since to You I belong.

More blue is the sky,
More brilliant the sun,
Since I met You,
Since I found the One.

Okay, a bit sappy, but I get it. Things look brighter when you know who Jesus is and what He has done. You see things through a different lens. So far, so good.

More delightful each day,
More restful each night,

More lovely each moment,
More spectacular each sight.

Screech! More restful each night? That hasn't always been my experience. There are times I've cried myself to sleep or lain awake in angst, asking God to give me strength or begging Him to heal a friend. Yes, He can give you peace during a tough time, but the pain is every bit as present.

The tenderness of Your touch
Ever do I feel,
Transcending my thought,
Yet ever true and real.

I agree, sometimes God is close. There have been times when His presence is so real to me, it is like I can reach out and touch Him. But I have to be honest: there are times—many times—when I can't feel the touch of God. He seems distant, and I can't seem to break through.

The music of Your voice
Resonates in all I hear,
Singing to my soul,
Ringing ever clear.

And there are times when I can't hear Him, either. I ask Him to show me His will, but He doesn't seem to answer. His voice, if He is speaking at all, is far away.

Surely all things are lovely
Since You and I did meet,
Surely all things

You make divinely sweet.[11]

All things are lovely? Not true. That school shooting was not lovely. The off-the-charts hunger in Burundi, Haiti, and Ethiopia is certainly not lovely. The fight I just overheard next door was not at all lovely. The devastation on families again and again by hurricanes and earthquakes surely isn't lovely. This is a really bad world sometimes, and everything doesn't look rosy just because I've met Jesus.

Some people treat following Jesus like a membership. It's like they think that since they have chosen to be on the Jesus team, they have a card in their wallet with certain privileges afforded them. Life will be easier. The paycheck will go farther. My boss will be nicer. Why? *Because Jesus and I are buds.*

I wish it were that easy. But I've been a follower of Jesus for a long time and will be the first to tell you all your problems don't just go away. You will still experience pain and struggles, and sometimes even an aching sense of worthlessness. You will still probably struggle to make good choices, and you will sometimes fall into patterns or habits you know are destructive but have been a lifelong battle.

When I was fourteen years old, I got a job mowing the lawn at my school. Workers had just cleared a huge field behind the building to convert it into a soccer field. After they planted the grass and it started growing, I was the first person to mow it.

The field was huge—probably a quarter mile in length. One day when I was mowing, I was having a terrible time trying to go in a straight line. I would drive the tractor in what I thought was a straight line, but when I turned around it looked like I had been trying to make a crescent moon shape.

My line was way off. I got off the tractor and stood there with my hands on my hips, trying to figure out why I couldn't drive that stupid tractor in a straight line.

Laverne Witt was my boss, and he saw me standing there looking puzzled and came out to assist. He looked at my work and could immediately see the problem. He taught me a lesson about mowing. . .and about life.

"If you want to go in a straight line, you need to fix your eyes all the way to the end of the field," he said. "Pick where you want to end up, and don't take your eyes off that point."

He was right. It worked perfectly. I would pick a tree in the distance, just beyond the edge of the field, and I would stare at it while driving straight toward it. I would get to the end and look back with pride: my line was perfectly straight. I followed that advice all through the summer. And anytime I started driving off course, it was always because I had stopped fixing my eyes on the end point.

The analogy is pretty obvious, isn't it? When I fix my eyes on Jesus, I stay on course. When I don't, then I don't have the strength or focus to do the next right thing. With my eyes on Jesus, I can respond well when I'm mistreated. With my eyes on Jesus, I can choose to show selfless love to my kids or my wife. Not only does He show me what love looks like, He gives me the strength to make the right choices and act on what I know.

Here's a good question to consider: Do you *trust* Jesus? Or do you just *know about* Jesus? We live in a world filled with people who know about Jesus. They have great respect for His teaching. They believe He was a good man. Some would even go as far as to say He was the greatest man who ever lived.

But they have not put their trust in Him. They have not made the decision to pursue Him and let Him impact every aspect of their lives. For them, Jesus is like the cross they wear around their neck. It dresses them up and makes them look good—but they take Him off when He's not convenient.

The Jesus-as-Jewelry people put on Jesus when they are in trouble and need advice. They take Him off when they are telling that small lie.

They put on Jesus when the house payment is overdue and they don't know where the money is going to come from. They take Him off when they are flirting with another guy's wife and hoping to score.

They put on Jesus when they go to church on Sunday. But they take Him off all the way home when they are gossiping and talking smack about the people they saw at church.

The Jesus-as-Jewelry types may even do good things for people. But so often they do it out of selfish motives. They want to look better in their friends' eyes or they feel the need to make up for staying out way too late and drinking way too much.

I'm not blaming the Jesus-as-Jewelry type of people. I'm not making fun of them, and I'm not condemning them. I get it. Jesus hasn't changed their lives. He is just someone they know *about*. Perhaps they even have seen His transforming power in someone else's life. They want it! *But not enough to give Him everything.*

It's the difference between "accepting Jesus as your Savior" (as though you are adding Him to your life like an Apple Watch) and giving Him everything so that His love transforms every corner of your life.

Some people choose to follow Jesus as a means to escape the fires of hell. Along the way, someone may have asked, "Do you know where you will go when you die?" If they said, "No" or "I'm not sure," then that question was probably followed up with the plan of salvation. Salvation from what? Well, hell of course.

Christians love the word *saved*. Maybe that's why it annoys me. I understand using the word when you are talking about money ("I saved $20") or chastity ("I saved myself for my wife")—but it grates on my nerves when I hear it in the Christian-ese context, as in "Is Johnny saved?" or "Let's pray that Martha gets saved."

It's not that I don't understand the context. Yes, I realize we sometimes need words to describe life after we meet Jesus. And, of course, I agree with the premise that there is something different about a person after he crosses the line of faith. It's just that I don't think the word *saved* is the right one.

For one, this word makes sense to insiders, but to the person who didn't grow up in church, it's just bad grammar: "Bob got saved." You wouldn't say of someone who was just rescued from drowning, "He got saved."

Beyond the grammar, when someone says, "I got saved in 1973," it is communicated as a once-and-for-all, passive event that happened *to* them. Like they did nothing at all. And once they get saved, they are good forever. I realize both of those things are true at their core. *Jesus paid it all, all to Him I owe*. But He requires me to accept the gift and give my life to Him. It's not something I did once (like becoming a citizen of a country); rather, it is the beginning of a journey in which I give my life to Him again every day.

But giving my life to Jesus is so much more than a fire escape. A life with Jesus is about changing the here and now. It's about working every day to see the kingdom of God established here on earth. . .today. It's not about biding my time until I get to be with Jesus after I die.

It would be like buying your eighteen-year-old his first car: a new Ford Shelby GT500 convertible. It has all the bells and whistles, and just for fun you put in the glove compartment a $50 gift card for the car wash. And for the next several years, your son never mentions the car but instead tells everyone he sees about the free car washes he got from his dad.

Did you get him free car washes? Yes, but that was just the icing on the cake. The real deal was the car.

I realize the analogy breaks down in that I'm comparing eternity with Jesus to a $50 gift card. My purpose isn't to downplay the eternal but to emphasize the importance of the here and now.

We sell Jesus and the Gospel short when we talk about our salvation story as simply being rescued from future damnation. Yes, you get to be with Jesus forever. But that's not the only reason Jesus forgave you and gave you new life.

Jesus rescued you so He could mark you with His love. He did that so you could bring "up there" down here, so you could show others who He is by your love for others.

Take the cheesy Christian bumper stickers off your car. That's not how people will know you follow Jesus. It is by your love!

Quit saying "praise Jesus" or "glory hallelujah" in every sentence as though they are conjunctions, and instead demonstrate your faith by your love.

Stop thinking about "winning souls" or inviting a friend to church so you can get another notch on your evangelistic belt, but instead look for ways to meet needs or help someone facing a crisis.

Marked by love. That is the sign of a Jesus follower. Does that describe your life?

12
STOP TALKING AND START LOVING

We went to lunch every month. Ted was a highly successful business owner who had recently come alive in his faith. By his own confession, until just a few years prior he had been coasting—not really serious about following Jesus. But something happened inside him, and now he was a new man—growing like a weed and trying to learn everything he could about how to make a difference in the world.

Our lunch conversations centered on work, family, faith, and the integration of it all. On this particular day, we sat down and placed our order. A few minutes later, the waitress, whose nametag read "Julie," came by to check on us and ask if there was anything she could do for us.

"Yes," Ted replied, "can you answer a question for me?"

I was only half paying attention, assuming he was going to change his order or ask her about a new menu item.

"I'll do my best," she kindly answered.

"What have you done with Jesus?" Ted asked.

No freaking way! Now I was paying attention. I think my face went instantly flush. I'm pretty sure I stared straight at my food and didn't look up. I was embarrassed. I was ashamed. I wanted to escape.

I could tell Julie was taken aback for a few seconds. Then she stammered a bit about how she didn't go to church and wasn't sure how to answer.

My friend was persistent. He wasn't mean, but he continued asking questions: "Do you think Jesus makes a difference in the world? Has Jesus ever made a difference in your life?"

A few different times, Julie tried to politely withdraw from this line of questioning. She had work to do and was demonstrably uncomfortable. Ted didn't seem to notice but eventually ended the conversation by inviting her to church, and then we went on with our meal.

I came back from that lunch meeting feeling disturbed. I wasn't sure why, but that interaction embarrassed me. I wanted to drive back to the restaurant and apologize to Julie. I could hear preacher voices in my head saying, "You must be embarrassed by Jesus." But I knew that wasn't true on that day. Nor is it today.

In my soul, I knew that wasn't the best way to help the Julies of the world. In fact, I was pretty certain it was more likely that Julie's view of Christians and Christianity had gone down a few notches. We had no relationship with Julie. Ted had not earned the right to be heard about something as intimate as faith and spirituality. We were taking advantage of Julie's obligation to listen. We were in *her* restaurant occupying one of *her* tables and keeping her from *her* other work.

It felt as awkward as the "bullhorn guy" we've all seen standing on the street in New York or Chicago or Los Angeles, the one shouting truth to people who have no reason to listen. You hear words like *repent*, *burn*, and *Jesus* in a seemingly insane tirade—but everyone just keeps walking. It has no relevance. This guy is just annoying.

I think it's interesting how often Jesus told people to keep quiet, as in "Don't tell anyone what I've done for you." Jesus often did miraculous, life-changing things in people's lives or families and then told them not to talk about it.

For example, one day Jesus healed two blind guys. We don't know how long they had been blind, but it was very likely their entire lives. Jesus touched their eyes and suddenly they could see. As Jesus walked away, He said, "See that no one knows about this" (Matthew 9:30 NIV).

First, I think it's funny that He started His sentence with "See." Two seconds ago, they were blind. But I digress.

Secondly, if I could make blind people see, I'd probably end my act with, "Thank you. . .thank you very much" (in my best Elvis voice). "Tell your friends. I'll be here all week."

Another time Jesus healed a guy with leprosy. You've likely never met anyone with leprosy, but, believe it or not, the disease still persists today.[12] It's an infectious disease that causes severe, disfiguring skin sores. It's actually not contagious, but people didn't know that in ancient times. Jesus healed the leper (as they were not very affectionately known), and his leprosy instantly disappeared. Imagine watching that! It would have rivaled Hollywood special effects to see his skin change instantly from being covered with hundreds of pus-oozing sores to being completely clear of any blemishes.

But then Jesus said, "Don't tell anyone about this." Instead, He told him to go see the priest, who could proclaim him healed. The guy was instantly healed, and he basically got procedural instructions: "Now that you are healed, you need to stop by the principal's office and get a pass so you can return to class" (see Matthew 8:1–4).

On another day, Jesus healed a man who was deaf and mute. He did this in front of a huge crowd and then told everyone in the crowd not to tell anyone (see Mark 7:35–36).

And then there was the time Jesus went into a house where a twelve-year-old girl had died. Within a few minutes, she was up walking around looking for something to eat, and Jesus told the family, "Don't tell a soul what just happened in this room" (see Mark 5:43).

This happened again and again and again. Jesus did something miraculous for someone—and then said, "Don't tell anyone."[13]

At the same time Jesus was running around healing people and telling them to keep quiet about it, He was also telling the crowds, "People will know you are my disciples by your love for one another." In another place, He says it this way: "This is my commandment, that you love one another as I have loved you. Greater love has no one than this, that someone lay down his life for his friends. You are my friends if you do what I command you" (John 15:12–14 ESV).

Two clear messages:

1. Don't tell anyone what I've done for you.
2. Love others. That's how people will know about Me.

I believe it is possible this is what Jesus was saying: love will change the world. When you live a life of love, people will sit up and take notice. They don't need another sermon or more information. They don't need to hear about how God changed your life back in 1973. People around you are facing loss and fear and disappointment and physical pain, and they need to know that they matter and that somebody cares. They need to experience an unnatural love from friends who will lay down their schedule, money, comfort, and more to make a tangible difference and give them hope to move forward.

What is going to be a stronger statement to a waitress—taking her away from her work to ask her about her soul and her relationship with Jesus, or treating her with grace and dignity, learning a bit about her story, and leaving a large tip? How many people just want something from her all day every day, including you with your Christian-ese questions, rather than trying to add value to her day and life?

What is going to be more memorable to a schoolteacher—the parent who only interacts with the staff when he believes his child has been wronged, or someone who comes alongside her like a partner, helps resource her with supplies, offers to volunteer in a way that is meaningful, and expresses love to that teacher?

What will more likely impact the guy you see nearly every day at Starbucks and who calls you by name and knows that you always order a grande caffè mocha with nonfat milk and no whipped cream? Is it when you treat him like a service-industry employee who owes you a product? Or is it when you call him by name, learn about what is important to him in this world, and go out of your way to communicate value and love?

There is an innate problem with starting a conversation with a stranger (someone with whom we have little or no relationship) about our faith or about Jesus, and it's this: we have no idea of the person's context or frame of reference.

If you ask ten people on the street who God is, what He expects of us, and how He deals with humans, you are likely to get ten different opinions. Even among those who self-identify as Christians, there are more than 33,000 denominations.[14] So, if people of faith have that many different opinions, imagine how many views exist among those who don't claim to be Christians!

If you ask people what they think about Jesus, they may instantly envision the anemic-looking, long-haired white guy with a suspicious smile they've seen in a picture on a wall somewhere. Or they might instantly remember the guy their parents said doesn't like it when they dance or wear tight clothes. Or they might picture the Jesus represented by Bullhorn Guy with the dirty placard that says "Repent or Burn!"

Without relationship and context, there is no common language. So stop leading with your mouth. Stop telling people they need Jesus, and instead show them they matter. Stop using fear or scare tactics and start loving. Stop talking and start showing. When the people God brings into your life begin to experience a truly giving, sacrificial, unconditional, authentic, and vulnerable love from you, it will have an impact.

In the movie *Evan Almighty*, God said: "How do you change the world? One act of random kindness at a time." On second thought, it was Morgan Freeman who said that—but it was inspired nonetheless. In fact, it was so profound that it prompted a student to drop out of college and start a nonprofit called Explore Kindness.[15] Alex Radelich, Dalton Lemert, and several of their buddies spent the next few years traveling all over the country in an RV doing random acts of kindness everywhere they went. They truly believed that showing love would change the world.

They did simple acts like giving away flowers on the street (one for you to keep, one for you to give away), purchasing presents for families in need, and spending time with kids at the children's hospital. Their mission—starting an epidemic of kindness—drove them to show love and encourage love.

And the world sat up and took notice. The young men were featured on the *Today Show*, on CBS News, in the *Huffington Post*, and in *USA Today*. Local television reporters in nearly every city they visited interviewed them. Why? *Because kindness is so rare.*

Lewie Clark is a lifelong friend who moved into the heart of Chicago several years ago. He started an organization focused on making disciples by following Jesus' approach.[16]

They meet needs, invite neighbors into their homes to share their stories and lives, and create a sense of belonging. Lewie recently said to me, "Love is the bridge to Jews, Muslims, and Hindus—and in their minds Christianity has nothing to do with love." In many ways, his dining-room table—not a pulpit or pew or building with a steeple—is the central hub for their teams' work.

What if this became the norm? What if we all saw love as the bridge? What if millions of self-proclaimed Christians began to operate from a place of love and compassion and care? What if our responses became unexpectedly loving? What if we took time to actually listen and care?

I might be crazy, but I actually believe love could change the world. Even as I say it, it sounds a bit cheesy. Maybe it sounds better if I quote the words of Peter:

> *Love each other as if your life depended on it. Love*
> *makes up for practically anything. Be quick to give a*
> *meal to the hungry, a bed to the homeless—cheerfully.*
> 1 Peter 4:8–9 msg

Who cares if it sounds cheesy? Let's start living it out and just see what happens.

13
A CHINESE MASSAGE

My friend Jim and I were in China. We were with a group who had come from different parts of America, met in Detroit, pretended to not know each other on the plane, and each smuggled a couple of suitcases of Bibles into mainland China. Miraculously, when we were ten feet away from the security checkpoint at the airport in Beijing, an old Chinese man dumped all his luggage right in front of us. The boxes split open, people began yelling, and in the commotion, we pushed our luggage carts right past the security guys with their machine guns. None of us was caught.

But that's not the story I want to tell.

Later that night, we had settled into our hotel in what appeared to be a seedy part of town. We were high off our recent experience and humbled that God had used us to deliver Bibles into a communist country. It had been a long trip, and we were very tired. That's when the phone rang. We answered, and a woman with a very kind and inviting voice said one word: "Massagie?" This happened many times every night, and we learned that this nice woman was offering to come up to our hotel room and give us personal massages. And no, not the professional, chiropractic type.

Throughout the trip, we saw women in the markets or on the street corners, making themselves available, especially to American men who likely had money to spend. On the outside, some of them were incredibly beautiful—hair perfect and skin glistening. But what hangs in my memory was one woman I saw standing near the booth where I was shopping. I noticed her body and her clothes. Her intentions were clear. But then I noticed her eyes. I didn't just look *at* her eyes—I looked *into* her eyes. And she looked into mine. For a couple of seconds that felt like minutes, our eyes were locked. And all I could see was a scared little girl, a girl who wanted to be loved, a girl who craved meaning and acceptance. Having daughters of my own, this stuck with me.

Of course, you don't have to go to China to find women who make their living off the pleasures of men. The options are abundant. It used to be you'd have to go to a convenience store and buy a magazine to feed your pornographic addiction. Then in the '70s you could actually bring a VHS tape home and watch *Debbie Does Dallas* in the privacy of your home. Beginning in the '80s and '90s you didn't even have to be seen at a video store—it was available through cable TV. A few years later, you had access from the desktop computer sitting in your office. Today, it's available on every phone and device you carry with you every minute of the day.

But really, nothing has changed. It still comes down to a choice we have to make every day, sometimes every minute: Will we act as though we are marked by love?

What would change if we looked at the women on the screen as treasures in the eyes of Jesus? What would change if we loved these young ladies as though they were as precious to us as our own wives or daughters? How would we love them if they were our best friend's daughter?

Do you ever wonder how Jesus would love a sexually

attractive woman known to be loose with her body? You don't have to guess—there is a story in the Bible about that exact scenario.

One day Jesus was eating in the home of a religious leader when a woman "known to be a harlot" came in and began worshipping at His feet. Literally. She knelt down, poured expensive perfume on His feet, and began washing them.

Some scholars say this perfume was worth a year's wages. Others say it was the most expensive perfume money could buy at the time. A quick Google search showed me that the most expensive perfume today is called Clive Christian No. 1 Imperial Majesty Perfume. It costs nearly $13,000 per ounce. It's likely not the type of perfume you would pour. You'd probably just use a drop at a time.

But this woman didn't dab it or use just a drop. She took the whole bottle and poured it on Jesus' feet. She was so caught up in the experience that she began crying and used her long hair to wipe her tears off His feet.

This woman had spent time in the company of many men, but never to wash their feet. This was an incredibly intimate act, but not the kind she was used to.

Simon, the dude who owned the home, was a bit put off by this interaction. He likely thought, *What the heck? If Jesus were really a prophet, He wouldn't let that filthy woman touch Him with a ten-foot pole.*

Simon's next thought should have been, *Oh crap! I forgot Jesus can read my mind.*

It would have been natural for Jesus to tell the woman to leave so that being so close to her would not harm His reputation. Or He could have chosen to rebuke her and condemn her lifestyle. It would have also been natural for Him to land on Simon's back with both feet and give him a verbal beating about his intolerance and judgmental heart.

Jesus did none of those things. Instead, He turned to Simon and told a very short story:

> *"Two men were in debt to a banker. One owed five hundred silver pieces, the other fifty. Neither of them could pay up, and so the banker canceled both debts. Which of the two would be more grateful?"*
>
> LUKE 7:41–42 MSG

It didn't seem complicated, and it didn't seem like a trick question. So Simon answered, "I suppose the one who was forgiven the most."

But Simon still didn't realize Jesus knew his thoughts—at least not until Jesus began giving him a lesson about love:

> *"That's right," said Jesus. Then turning to the woman, but speaking to Simon, he said, "Do you see this woman? I came to your home; you provided no water for my feet, but she rained tears on my feet and dried them with her hair. You gave me no greeting, but from the time I arrived she hasn't quit kissing my feet. You provided nothing for freshening up, but she has soothed my feet with perfume. Impressive, isn't it? She was forgiven many, many sins, and so she is very, very grateful. If the forgiveness is minimal, the gratitude is minimal."*
>
> LUKE 7:44–47 MSG

You know what I think are the most important words in this passage? *"Then turning to the woman, but speaking to Simon. . ."*

Can you picture this? As was typical in those days, Jesus was sitting on the floor at a table. This wasn't a dining-room table with chairs, like where you might eat a Thanksgiving meal. No, this was more like the short tables in a preschool classroom—no chairs or benches. Jesus was on the floor, His feet behind Him and to the side. The woman was on her knees, behind Jesus, washing His feet. She was ashamed and lowered herself to the point of kissing Jesus' feet. They had not yet locked eyes.

Not until this very moment, that is. Now Jesus looked directly into her eyes. He saw everything she had ever done. He immediately knew every detail of her life. She looked back, and she knew that He knew. She didn't know *how* He knew, but she was sure He knew. And yet, He looked at her with such grace and love and acceptance. The words He spoke to Simon were for Simon, but they were for her as well. He didn't talk about the men she'd been with, the unspeakable acts she had done, or the places she'd done them. He didn't suggest that she probably got the perfume as a gift from one of her many "clients."

None of that came up. He just looked at her with the most caring and loving eyes she had ever seen—and in those eyes she saw no want or lust or disapproval. As she gazed, wanting to turn away but unable, she was sure she would never forget those eyes.

And if that wasn't enough, she listened to the words He spoke to Simon. Wait, what? He told Simon, a well-known religious leader, about *her* good works. He praised her to Simon, expressing thanks for the way she had shown her love by washing His feet. In fact, He even used her as an example as He scolded Simon for his lack of love. This couldn't be! She had never been praised as an example of anything, and yet Jesus spoke these words. Such love!

He ended His talk, and then, while continuing to look at her, He spoke directly into her soul, saying the words she had longed her whole life to hear: "I forgive your sins."

I can't prove this, but I believe love may be the most powerful sin deterrent on the planet. It is stronger than reading your Bible, praying, or memorizing scripture (although all those activities can help keep you from sin). It is stronger than knowing something is wrong or rehearsing the shame that will come with getting caught. Love, when fully accepted, is the antidote for sin.

It seems like Christians have an obsession with sex, especially when it comes to our kids and teens. Sexual activity (or refraining from it) has become the one litmus test for holiness and right living. But our repeated attempts at controlling our kids' environments so they won't "hook up" has the same magnetic appeal as a bench with a "Don't Touch, Wet Paint" sign attached. While we focus on a specific physical activity, we oftentimes neglect our children's hearts. We may be able to control their time (and thus their zippers) for a while, but in the meantime, they become bitter, angry, greedy, lustful, dishonest, and ungrateful.

C. S. Lewis said it this way in *Mere Christianity*:

> *The center of Christian morality has little to do with sex. If anyone thinks that Christians regard unchastity as the supreme vice, he is quite wrong. The sins of the flesh are bad, but they are the least bad of all sins. All the worst pleasures are purely spiritual: the pleasure of putting other people in the wrong, of bossing and patronizing and spoiling sport, and backbiting; the pleasure of power, of hatred.*[17]

I think we should take notes from Jesus, who didn't talk about premarital sex or pornography, but who talked quite a bit about love. What if we focused more on love and less on sex?

I have a friend who began praying for the man who would

become her husband when she was in high school. It was this focused prayer that kept her pure in body and mind. How could she not save her body for the man for whom she had been praying all these years—even before she knew him?

What if we began praying for the women in the porn industry? What if we asked, "How would God love them?" What if, instead of condemning them, we took a cue from Jesus and instead loved on them? What if we pictured their dads and moms, who are probably heartsick and wondering if their little girls are okay?

What if the obsession we expressed with our teens was on how to love God and love others fully? What if we focused on ways to love every person we meet—and less on the rules?

I would be lying if I said I have never struggled with lust. This is the world we live in. More than 90 percent of boys and 60 percent of girls are exposed to porn before they turn eighteen years old.[18] If you don't wrestle with lust, you are in a very small minority.

I can remember lying in my bed at night as a nineteen- or twenty-year-old man and begging God to take away my sexual desires. I didn't understand why God would give me such strong, seemingly uncontrollable urges and then tell me I couldn't fulfill them. It seemed like putting a piece of steak in a cage with a hungry bulldog and expecting it to still be uneaten the next morning. What kind of cruel God would do that?

At the time, the only possible explanation I could think of was that God gave me my sexual desire to teach me self-control. As the Buddhist believes, if I deny myself something so great, I will grow closer to God. But that doesn't sound much like a God of grace, does it?

What if it's *not* God trying to be cruel? What if it's *not* a harsh lesson in self-control? What if God gave me sexual desires to teach me about His love? God has prewired me with certain urges and desires. He put me on this planet and gave me the privilege of interacting with women—the most beautiful of His creation. So how will I deal with my sexual impulses?

The answer is to run every thought, desire, urge, impulse, and activity through a filter of love. In dating, do my decisions honor this girl and her future husband? How would Jesus love her? If I were to walk up to her new husband on their wedding day, could I say, "I treated your wife with love and respect and honor. I have no regrets"?

In marriage, do I love my wife and my kids in every sexual decision? Is my spouse getting 100 percent of me sexually? Or is my sexual energy and attention being diverted or reserved for only myself?

Am I doing anything to minimize my ability to fully love my spouse? Am I looking at anything that diminishes my capacity to view others as treasured daughters or sons of God?

Bottom line: Am I behaving as though I am marked by the love of God? Am I looking at others as though they are marked by love?

Love could make the difference. It's not a once-and-for-all-take-this-pill-and-you'll-be-fixed deal. But if I choose to live in His love for this one hour, asking "How would Jesus love. . ." at every opportunity, there is a better chance I'll be living in His love two hours from now. And if I live in His love a couple of hours from now, there is a good chance I'll make it through the day living in the power of His love. And if I adjust my life as though I'm marked by His love for an entire day, I might make it for a week. And pretty soon, it begins to make a difference in my choices.

In fact, after a while, I might just start looking like a disciple.

14
HAPPY HOLIDAYS

In my opinion, there should be a rule about Christmas music. It should be illegal to play it until the day after Thanksgiving, and once December ends, it should no longer be allowed. That is me being generous; my personal preference would be to narrow that window to about three weeks. (Oh, and Christmas music with a country twang should be outlawed, period. No exceptions.)

God had a sense of humor when He thought of this thing called marriage, because Faith (my wife) is exactly the opposite of me on this topic. She starts humming Christmas music shortly after the Fourth of July, begins looking at her Christmas playlist on Labor Day, and is playing Christmas music full blast by Halloween. Somewhere around Valentine's Day she gets depressed as she begins thinking about the possibility of the thought of putting her Christmas music away. Usually, somewhere between Easter and Mother's Day, she ceases playing the holiday music and we bring our nine-month Christmas season to a close. I should also mention that at least 25 percent of her tunes are of the "country" variety—something about a pickup truck, a dog, a bad relationship, and a partridge in a pear tree.

I'm also not a big hymn guy, so my toes tend to curl up when I hear a Christmas song that is hundreds of years old and fashioned like a hymn. Nothing wrong with those songs, I just don't personally like them. (If you see me at a Christmas service with my eyes rolled back and head drooping, it's not because I've had a stroke. The music actually put me to sleep).

I will admit, I find some of the newer Christmas music much more tolerable. I have a twenty-year-long shtick to uphold of not liking Christmas music, so don't tell my family, but I really do enjoy some of the newer tunes.

A few years back, I walked into the house to hear a new-to-me Christmas song. Go Fish is a group that specializes in Christian music for kids, and they had produced a fun song called "Christmas with a Capital 'C.'" It begins by telling a story about a man going to the coffee shop to get a drink. But it quickly takes a turn when the barista has the nerve to wish him "Happy Holidays" instead of "Merry Christmas."

Sometime in the early 2000s, just before this song was written, a huge debate had started in the US that became known as the "War on Christmas." (Truth be told, the *war* actually began long before that. In the 1800s, it was the Christians who banned Christmas because it had no grounding in the Bible. But I digress.) Since then, the war has taken on many different "enemies," including government buildings, schools, Communists, Muslims, and, more recently, retailers.

When Amazon proclaimed to its shoppers, "Happy Holidays," a grassroots effort galvanized to make them change or take them down. Throughout the ensuing decade, boycotts and marketing efforts were taken against Sears, Walmart, Target, Best Buy, and others with the goal of inflicting economic pain on the giant retailers if they didn't reconsider their stance against this Christian holiday.

Bill O'Reilly, the highest-rated evening news personality

at that time, became the spokesman for this effort, with the American Family Association coordinating the marketing for the boycotts. Focus on the Family contributed by publishing lists of "Christmas-friendly," "Christmas-negligent," and "Christmas-offensive" retailers.[19]

Evangelicals and conservatives banded together. We had powerful media on our side. And guess what? It worked. In 2005, Sears reversed its policy and began saying "Merry Christmas" again. In 2006, Walmart relented; Target also changed its position after a petition containing 700,000 signatures was circulated; Home Depot and Gap followed soon after and changed their positions in 2008 and 2009, respectively.[20]

We'd been told if we didn't win, the country would fall to socialism and moral ambiguity—and that's how the German people accepted the Nazis, so it was a war we had to win. The very survival of America depended on it. And boom! We won. Oh, there are still boycotts every year and retailers are still being challenged. (Starbucks even got in trouble a couple of years ago for excluding snowflakes or reindeer on their plain red cup.) But put a check mark in the Christian column. In your face, retailers! Up yours, liberal media! We are on the winning side!

As "Christmas with a Capital 'C' " continues into its bridge, a not-quite-rap, sort-of-preachy sermon is shouted to listeners. It's obvious the writer is ticked off at the barista for offending his Christian values. In essence, he says, "You don't have to believe in Christmas, but get used to it, because America is a Christian nation. I don't care if it offends you, I'm going to keep saying it!"

And all God's people cheer and laugh from the safety of our perfectly lined rows of pews in churches across America. Whipped into a frenzy, feeling the superiority of having made our point and beaten our enemies, we high-five each other and offer a smile and feeling of satisfaction.

We won.

Or did we? Sure, the greeter at Walmart can now say "Merry Christmas" again. But did we really win?

While trying to recover our cultural right to have all of society acknowledge our beliefs, this is what everyone else hears:

> *This is a Christian nation! You can't take it over. It's ours! We don't care about Muslims or Africans or atheists—they can say what they want in their country. But America is ours!*

Meanwhile, single moms and struggling retirees and ambitious college students work for an hourly wage during the Christmas season for a few extra dollars to feed their kids or take care of a sick family member or pursue their dreams. They aren't impressed that the boycott worked. No, they are out of work now and more certain than ever that Christianity is a religion of bigotry and intolerance.

Millions who watch the debate unfold on national TV every year during the Christmas season hear religious leaders passionately, almost angrily, defend the "right" of Christians to keep their holiday and have the world recognize it. The same holiday we preach about as having become too commercialized—it suddenly makes a difference to us that those commercial entities acknowledge in their marketing that they are selling us goods because of the birth of Christ.

And the world watches, and it wonders. They don't see us talking with the same level of passion about feeding the hungry or providing warm shelter for the homeless. The stuff in the world that really matters barely gets a mention, but don't even think about buying your 4K TV from a store that won't put "Merry Christmas" on its sign—because that violates your rights!

So, I ask, where is the love? If we are disciples of Jesus, marked by love, where is the love evident as we yell at the world because it won't acknowledge one of our traditions?

If I am marked by love, would I really be offended if someone sincerely greets me with "Happy Holidays" instead of "Merry Christmas"? If I am marked by love, wouldn't I care more than I do about the Muslims, Jews, Jehovah's Witnesses, atheists, or even some sects of Christianity who don't celebrate the holiday?

If I am marked by love, would I really care whether my bank sends me a holiday greeting rather than a Christmas card? Is it really worth changing banks, walking away from the relationship I've built with one of the tellers, just to make a point?

If I am marked by love, would I act as though this is "my" country, and you must respect "my" values?

I'm not sure where it started, but we American Christians have a corporate sense of entitlement. Herb Silverman, a self-described atheist, wrote in the *Washington Post*, "Could it be that many Christians lament the possibility that their dominance and privilege in America might be nearing an end?"[21]

He might be right. We think everyone is supposed to be nice to us. We expect society to treat us well, to give us preferential treatment, to put us in the front of the line. After all, there are more of us. We deserve special treatment.

And yet Jesus preached about an entirely different kind of approach: "Blessed are you when people hate you, when they exclude you and insult you and reject your name as evil, because of the Son of Man" (Luke 6:22 NIV).

It would probably be presumptuous, maybe even ignorant, to think this verse applies to the "War on Christmas." If crucifixion is a +100 on the persecution scale, then hearing my Applebee's server say "Happy Holidays" is somewhere around a 0.0000001.

And yet I think the principle is still very much the same. If you align your life with Jesus, people are going to say things about you, your "rights" will be stomped on, you won't be included in everything, and they may even twist the facts to make you look like the bad guy.

So how do you handle some of these hot topics? What do you do when society tries to get you to take a side? How do you reply when a coworker, who knows you are a Christian, tries to get you to defend the publicly held but judgmental Christian viewpoint on a topic? How about when you see your Facebook feed blowing up over an issue, and well-intentioned followers of Jesus respond in mean and insulting ways to people who don't agree?

I think we get an answer to these questions when we see what Jesus said right *before* He talked about persecution. In Matthew's account of the same sermon, Jesus said, "You're blessed when you can show people how to cooperate instead of compete or fight. That's when you discover who you really are, and your place in God's family" (Matthew 5:9 MSG).

For a few weeks every December, we have an opportunity. What better time than Christmas to show the love of Jesus? What better opportunity to be disciples, marked by love, than when we are surrounded by people bickering over a store's marketing plan?

Dr. Russell D. Moore wrote these words regarding the war on Christmas:

> *We ought not to get outraged by all that, as though we were some protected class of victims. We ought to instead see the ways that our culture is less and*

less connected with the roots of basic knowledge about Christianity. . .that ought not make us angry. It ought to instead give us an opportunity to understand how we look to our neighbors. They see us more in terms of our trivialities than in terms of the depths of meaning of Incarnation and blood atonement and the kingdom of Christ. They know something about "Silent Night," just as they know something about "Grandma Got Run Over by a Reindeer." What they don't recognize is the cosmos-shifting mystery of Immanuel as God with Us.

All that means is that we need to spend more time lovingly engaging our neighbors with the sort of news that shocks angels and redirects stargazers and knocks sheep-herders to the ground. That it seems increasingly strange is all the better—because it is strange. A gospel safe enough to sell beer and barbecue grills is a gospel too safe to make blessings flow.[22]

That's called love. And our world needs a good dose.

15
THE NEXT PERSON

Christmas is supposed to be a happy time of the year. And it is for many people. But the holidays aren't immune from pain and tragedy. And tragedy is exactly what happened on Christmas Eve in 2008.

Gene Ort had attended an early Christmas Eve service with his granddaughter. I don't know if I saw him that afternoon, but I do know I often saw him at church. Gene is always smiling, joking around, and encouraging others. I'm guessing he was doing the same on this particular day.

After the service, Gene headed to his aunt's house in the nearby town of Cassopolis, Michigan. The family was gathered for their traditional Christmas Eve meal. Everyone that is, except Rachel, who had not yet arrived.

Rachel was the twenty-six-year-old daughter of Gene and Mary. I had only met Rachel a couple of times, but when I did, it wasn't hard to believe she was Gene's daughter. The way he described her: "Rachel lit up a room when she walked in. It was like the Fourth of July. She was such a bright and loving person, and it just shone in everything she did. It was contagious to be around. It was magical."

At seven thirty that evening, Gene and Mary started to

worry. It wasn't like Rachel to be this late. Mary turned to Gene and said, "Rachel's not here. Go find your daughter."

Gene left the house, and within minutes he came upon his worst nightmare. Flashing lights, ambulances, fire trucks.

I can identify with that gut-wrenching feeling. Soon after one of my daughters started driving, I received the dreaded phone call: "Your daughter has been in a car accident. You need to come now." I had been dropped off at the office that day and didn't have a car. As I ran to the parking lot, I saw a friend and said, "I need your car keys. Now!" I jumped in his car and raced to the scene of the accident, all the while my heart racing and my mind jumping to the worst possible outcome.

I came over the crest of a hill and saw that emergency vehicles had blocked off the entire five-lane road. There were at least ten different ambulances, fire trucks, and police cars blocking the road. And blocking my view of the accident.

My day ended with me holding Megan in my arms while she cried, bruised and scared, but very much alive.

Gene's day ended differently. He drove past the barricade, past the first few emergency vehicles, and right up to the accident site, where he immediately recognized Rachel's car. He got out to head for the car, but an officer stopped him.

"Is she dead?" he asked. But before he got an answer, he fell to the ground in complete devastation. He knew. Rachel had not survived the crash.

If you have lost anyone close, you know that the coming days and weeks and months for Gene and his family were the darkest and most difficult they had ever faced.

Gene described it this way: "The days following the accident might be, it's easy to say, the worst time period in my life. I had no idea something could hurt this bad and have no wound. It's not just your pain you are dealing with, it's the pain of everyone around you. It's compounded. And you just can't imagine ever being right again."

I recently had the opportunity to hear Gene tell his story about losing Rachel. He talked about going back to work for the first time after the accident:

> *A couple weeks went by and it was time to go back to work. At least that's what I thought. I really didn't want to engage with people too much, so I went back to my office and closed my door. I will admit I had no desire to be there. Nothing had any meaning to me anymore. And I said it out loud, "What am I supposed to do now?"*
>
> *And I got an answer. This was internal, this wasn't external, but God said my name, "Gene, this is what I want you to do. I want you to love Me, I want you to love yourself, and I want you to love the next person I put in front of you. And just keep doing that."*[23]

I hope you didn't read that too quickly. If so, read it again.

Gene felt God saying to him: "Love Me. Love yourself. Love the next person I put in front of you. And just keep doing that."

It was a message for Gene, but also one for all of us.

After I heard Gene tell this story, I couldn't stop thinking about it. It is simple. It is profound. It could be a game changer. And quite possibly, it could change the world. Imagine if every person on planet Earth who claims to follow Jesus would just do those three things:

1. Love God.
2. Love yourself.

3. Love the next person you see.

Perhaps it holds power and grabs our hearts because it is exactly what Jesus said over and over again. The Bible's word for "the next person you see" is *neighbor*. And over and over we are challenged with these words: *Love your neighbor*.

All the way back in Leviticus, in a long list of instructions God gave to Moses for the people of Israel, He includes: "Don't seek revenge or carry a grudge against any of your people. Love your neighbor as yourself. I am GOD" (Leviticus 19:18 MSG).

And you thought Leviticus was boring and irrelevant! In Romans, Paul talks about this same idea:

> *The commandments, "You shall not commit adultery,"*
> *"You shall not murder," "You shall not steal," "You*
> *shall not covet," and whatever other command there*
> *may be, are summed up in this one command: "Love*
> *your neighbor as yourself." Love does no harm to a*
> *neighbor. Therefore love is the fulfillment of the law.*
> ROMANS 13:9–10 NIV

My favorite part of this verse is the words "and whatever other command there may be." That is the first-century version of saying "yada, yada, yada." Like this:

> *You know the commands—don't commit adultery,*
> *don't murder, don't steal, don't covet, yada, yada,*
> *yada. All those rules can be summed up in one: Love*
> *your neighbor as yourself. . . .*

Wait, every commandment can be summed up in one? Yeah, all of them. There isn't one "rule" in the Bible that doesn't fit under "love your neighbor."

- *Don't steal.*
- *Don't have sex with someone you aren't married to.*
- *Don't gossip.*
- *Don't murder.*
- *Be just.*
- *Don't seek revenge.*
- *Respect the elderly.*
- *Be honest in your business dealings.*

Every rule applies to how you treat others. So the big question is, "Who is my neighbor?"

I'm glad you asked.

16
WHO IS MY NEIGHBOR?

I could start this chapter with an analogy about Mister Rogers and how he wants to be your neighbor. But half of you would have no idea who I'm talking about. Just trust me when I say Mr. Rogers took off his cardigan sweater for the last time years ago and can no longer be your neighbor, so we have to figure this out.

To do that, we need look no further than a story in the Bible told by a medical doctor named Luke. He told of a day when an attorney (let's call him Frank) came to Jesus and sincerely asked, "I want to live forever. How do I do that?"

Instead of answering, Jesus turned it around and basically said, "Frank, you know the Bible. What do you think the answer is?"

Frank had likely heard Jesus teaching because he answered with the same exact answer Jesus had given on a few occasions: "Love God with all your heart, soul, strength, and mind. And love your neighbor as yourself."

So far, so good. But that really isn't the question or the answer Frank was looking for. He already knew he was supposed to love God and love his neighbor. Frank wanted to take it a step further. Perhaps he was trying to justify some questionable business negotiations or back-alley deals with clients. Perhaps he was in a domestic dispute with his in-laws or fighting with city officials over property rights.

We don't know exactly what was behind Frank's next question: "But he wanted to justify himself, so he asked Jesus, 'And who is my neighbor?'" (Luke 10:29 NIV).

Who is my neighbor? That's a great question.

Some of my earliest memories of neighbors come from when I lived on Ash Drive. We moved there when I was about seven years old, and we stayed there until I graduated high school. I remember the Thorne family, whose backyard backed up next to ours. Mr. Thorne was very tall, and Mrs. Thorne very motherly. I remember my friend Jimmy Carter, who lived two doors down. It was awesome to have a buddy with the same name as the current president. Mr. Leonard lived right next door. He was so nice to me. One day he had a stroke, and after that I would go over and sit with him for a couple of hours at a time. He would ask me the same questions over and over.

As an adult, my wife and I lived in the same home for nearly twenty years. The Andersons, Richardses, Derbys, Pottschmidts, and Janickis were our neighbors for the better part of two decades. So many memories, so many life happenings.

So, is that who Jesus is talking about when He said to "love your neighbor"? Was He talking about the people who live in the house next to you and across the street? Well yes, kind of, but not completely.

Jesus answered Frank's question by telling a story. (So predictable, right?)

In order to illustrate the story and make it a bit more

relatable—I'm going to tell the story as Jesus might have told it two thousand years later. Let's pretend it is the 1960s, and Jesus is telling this story in Alabama. It might go something like this:

> *A white man was driving from Montgomery to Birmingham when he was carjacked. The perpetrators took everything he had, including the clothes he was wearing, and beat him unconscious, leaving him nearly dead on the side of the road.*
>
> *A white priest drove up, saw the beaten man lying helplessly on the shoulder of the highway, but he continued driving, pretending not to notice. Another religious leader did the same thing.*
>
> *Then a black man drove up, saw the dying, naked white man lying in the street—and he stopped and got out to help. He picked him up and took care of him, tending to his wounds with bandages and ointment. He drove him to the next town and put him up in a hotel—staying with him overnight.*
>
> *The next day the black man had to leave. But he gave the hotel manager $150 and said, "Look after him, and when I return I'll reimburse any additional expenses you might have."*

In Jesus' version of the story, He used the Jews and the Samaritans. These two groups hated each other. The Samaritans were people of a different race, different nationality, and rival religions. Perhaps a more current version would be Islamic extremists and fundamentalist Christians. Whatever analogy you prefer, Jesus purposely told a story in which a Samaritan ended up being the hero.

In Jesus' story, two Jewish men, a priest and a Levite, passed by a man who had been beaten nearly to death, but a Samaritan stopped to help him.

Jesus had a knack for telling stories that made people feel uncomfortable. Imagine the discomfort of the Jews listening to this story. He ended the story by asking Frank, "Which of these three do you think was a neighbor to the injured man?"

Frank didn't download his college degree off the internet. He was a smart man, and he answered, "The one who had mercy on him."

Jesus affirmed his answer and said, "Go and do the same."

Was He saying, "Go and be a good neighbor to someone who is of a different race than you?" No, yes, kind of, not really, but yes.

He was making the point that your neighbor is anyone and everyone you meet, see, or come in contact with. Your neighbor is the woman at the cash register; your neighbor is the man walking his dog, who you pass when you are out running; your neighbor is the homeless man begging on the side of the road, who you pass every day on your way to lunch; your neighbor is that annoying coworker you can't believe hasn't been fired yet.

God told Gene Ort: *Love the next person I put in front of you.*

He tells us the same thing.

John Ortberg said it this way,

> *Jesus says you are to love your neighbor. Not a cause.*
> *Not some abstract group of marginalized people*
> *who are conveniently located on the other side of*
> *the globe, someplace real far away, where I'll never*

actually have to be put out by coming into contact with them. Your neighbor is the real flesh and blood, imperfect, difficult person that life brings you into contact with.[24]

Jesus said the two greatest commandments are to (1) love God and (2) love your neighbor. But these are not actually two commandments. You cannot love God without loving others. And you cannot truly love others if you haven't experienced the love of God in your own life. As the apostle John wrote, "We love because he first loved us" (1 John 4:19 NIV).

Loving God is a bit intangible, a bit mystical, a bit hard to measure. How can anyone see people's hearts and know if they really love God? I'll tell you how. You see people's love for God in how much they love others:

- How do they treat others?
- How do they talk about others?
- How do they respond when they learn about the need of others?
- How selfless are they?
- How do they celebrate others' successes?
- How do they invest their time and money in others?

Your love for God is not measured by how often you go to church. Your love for God is not measured by how high you raise your hands when you are singing. It's not about how many times you read the Bible each week or whether you cross yourself or if you pray for hours every day. To the degree those things help you become more loving toward your neighbor, then they are good. But to the degree they keep you from loving others, they stand between you and a right relationship with God and should be stopped.

Love God.

How?

By loving others. Start with the next person you see. And keep doing that.

17
THE PRINCIPLE OF PROXIMITY

Think about this:

> *It is more my responsibility to care for people around me than it is the responsibility of those who are far away.*

> *And, I have a greater responsibility to care for those I'm close to than I do for those I am not close to.*

These statements are similar, but different. Read them again.

Let me say this another way, using as an example Hurricane Harvey and the subsequent flooding that impacted the city of Houston, where I live:

> *Because I live in Houston, it is more my responsibility to care for those who are flooded nearby than it is the responsibility of others who live far away.*

> *And, I have a greater responsibility to care for those who live on my street than I do to care for those who live in Utah or Canada or Zimbabwe.*

God so loved the world, but I am to love my neighbor. Jesus healed people in front of Him. There were probably hundreds of thousands of sick and crippled and diseased people alive when Jesus walked the earth—and yet the ones He healed were the ones He actually met.

Sometimes the excessive needs in the world overwhelm us and shut us down. And we do nothing. I'm suggesting you don't need to focus on the needs of the world. That is God's job. Just focus on the ones in front of you—the ones you know about and that He can use you to meet.

My neighbors became my responsibility as soon as I moved into the neighborhood. The day I was born, it became my responsibility to care for, love, and encourage my family and to meet their needs. When they face a crisis, I face a crisis. When they have a need, if it is within my power, I am to help meet the need.

Like the Good Samaritan, there will be times when I cross paths with a needy someone I have never met. At that moment, the principle of proximity compels me to see if and how I can meet a need. Every time I walk into the grocery store or am sitting in a waiting room at the doctor's office, the people around me become my neighbors. The principle of proximity reminds me to keep my antenna up and watch for ways I can love others through listening, encouraging, or meeting a tangible need.

Because of the principle of proximity, Faith and I set aside a percentage of our money every month to make it available to meet other people's needs. When we find that someone has a need, we don't have to sell stuff or stop paying our mortgage—we are ready to respond. That doesn't mean we give money away loosely and without thought. It still requires conversation and discernment.

You might be thinking, *Well, if we all operated that way,*

no one would ever help the people in India or Sudan, because we would never be in close proximity to those people.

Sometimes God will compel you to meet a faraway need. God calls some to lead charities, to join mission agencies, to serve in humanitarian efforts, or to start a company like TOMS to meet the needs of those who live on the other side of the world.

Each of us can find a local church or other credible charitable organization to support. Giving in this way allows a community of people to pool their resources and help meet needs of people they will never know. It is how our family has helped plant churches and drill wells and train children in southern India. It is how we were able to help with disaster relief in Haiti, Puerto Rico, and Florida. The principle of proximity would never have made it possible for me to help in those locations. But my commitment to live in community through a local church that is committed to meeting needs outside its four walls, or my intentional support of a high-impact charity, enables me to also help people way outside my location.

Sometimes we look in awe at the people who single-handedly do huge works for good. Recently, J. J. Watt (star player for the NFL's Texans and a hometown hero in Houston) sent out a tweet and raised $37 million for hurricane recovery efforts. Okay, that's pretty awesome.

Bill and Melinda Gates set up a foundation to make the world a better place. They have personally donated more than $28 billion to the foundation to help control infectious diseases and meet basic nutrition and sanitation needs, among other initiatives. That was the largest single donation in the history of the world.

If I just had J. J. Watt's spotlight status or Bill Gates's money, then I could do a lot of good. I could make a huge difference. Right?

Sometimes we get paralyzed because we think we can't make a difference. We think our little contribution won't help. But nothing could be further from the truth. Your random act of kindness can make the difference in someone's life. It makes a difference when you listen to someone's story, when you meet the need of a neighbor, when you write a note of encouragement, when you smile and extend love to someone who doesn't particularly deserve it.

In 1988, George H. W. Bush famously talked about a "thousand points of light." He said it isn't about the United States government meeting the world's needs—it's about each of us all doing something. It's about everyone jumping in and helping their neighbor. It's about volunteering for the food pantry down the street and housing that family that was displaced from their home.

You can't do everything. But you can do something.

You can't meet the needs of the whole world. But you can meet somebody's needs.

You can't personally show love to the whole world. But you can show love to the family who lives next door.

Start doing something. Start today.

18
THREE GIRLS AND A RUMOR

Madge Rodda is probably someone you can picture quite easily. She is an older woman who reads her Bible every day, goes to church, and for years was the organist for her congregation. The typical grandma, right?

Maybe not. One of her dear friends is James Bridle. Theirs is an unlikely friendship, not just because of the nearly fifty year age difference, but because Bridle tried to rape and kill her in a Denny's bathroom when she was seventy years old.

Every Sunday morning, Madge would drive to Denny's to read her Bible and eat breakfast before heading to church in Costa Mesa, California.

Except on this particular day, she wouldn't make it to church. As she was leaving the restaurant, she stopped to use the restroom. Hiding in the stall next to her was Bridle, high on cocaine, looking at a pornographic magazine, and waiting with a knife for whoever would come in next.

The attack was violent and extended. According to news reports, Bridle "choked her, bashed her head repeatedly on the tile floor, cut her throat, and tried to sexually assault her." Although she was less than five feet tall and weighed barely one hundred pounds, Madge Rodda fought back with a vengeance against her twenty-three-year-old attacker.

Though no one heard her, she screamed over and over for God to save her. After Bridle finished the assault, he told his beaten and bloodied victim, "I believe in God too. But Satan is poisoning my mind. I need help. I know I need help."

Bridle fled the restaurant but was apprehended minutes later. Madge Rodda's life was saved, and she was rushed to a nearby hospital.

Although she had difficulty speaking, she was able to utter these words to her daughter immediately after the attack: "That poor man. That poor man. We must find a way of getting him a Bible."

The *Los Angeles Times* reported it this way:

> *Not a lot of people understood what she was doing.*
> *The rape counselors insisted she was in denial and*
> *pleaded with her to "get [her] anger out." Others*
> *thought she was a saint, a theory Rodda laughs at.*
>
> *"It's my nature to hold a grudge," Rodda said. "I*
> *can remember things from years and years ago that*
> *everyone else has probably forgotten."*
>
> *Rodda's explanation is simply that the spirit*
> *of God moved her. "This wasn't natural, it was*
> *supernatural," Rodda said.*
>
> *And so Rodda forgave James Bridle. They*
> *met again for the first time in court. After a judge*
> *sentenced Bridle to seventeen years in prison—which*
> *Rodda thought was fair—she gave her assailant a*
> *Bible with verses she had highlighted to help him on*
> *his spiritual journey.*
>
> *"God knew this attack was going to happen,"*
> *Rodda said. "So he sent a little old lady organist*
> *who'd have no better sense than to stand up in court*

*with a Bible and say to her attacker, 'The word of
God is all you need.'"*

*And so began an unusual relationship between
a victim and her attacker. She's visited him in jail,
they've written each other letters, she's sent gifts and
now they call each other friend.*[25]

This type of forgiveness is unnatural. It is unexpected. It is
newsworthy because it is so rare.

Madge Rodda says it this way: "You may not feel forgiveness, compassion, and love, but God will always provide the
grace for us to do what He has commanded us to do, and He
has commanded us to forgive."

Forgive. That is a difficult teaching.

My enemies aren't as extreme. No one has tried to kill me.
No one has taken the life of one of my children. No one has
tried to burn down my house.

But I have been wronged. People have tried to hurt me.
And when that happens, I have a choice to make: will I
respond in love or will I choose to hold that grudge?

Many years ago, an email was accidentally sent to me.
Three friends (all women, two of them close friends of me
and my wife) had been talking about me via email. It was vile.
It was hurtful.

"Something is wrong with him."

"He has problems."

It was a twisted exchange of gossip, accusations, and
conjecture. I was crushed. I had been stabbed in the back by
good friends, and I felt pain so deep it was hard to describe
to anyone.

Because two of the women worked at my office, I immediately showed it to my boss. They had attacked my integrity,
and I didn't have the objectivity to confront it myself. I was

mad. I was hurt. As far as I knew, I had done nothing to any of them or to anyone else.

With my boss present, I talked to each of the women. I asked for specifics in where I had hurt them. I wanted to know what I needed to do in order to strengthen my character. They each admitted there was nothing specific. I had done nothing wrong. They confessed to gossip and slander and said their conversation got out of hand. They said they were sorry.

Sorry. A word easily said but not easily received. "Sorry" didn't take away the deep wound. I uttered the words "I forgive you," but in my heart I was still hanging on. Over the coming months, I would pull out the emails every few weeks and relive the pain. Like a child picking at a scab, I kept the wound very much open. Every time I read the emails, I would get mad again.

About a year later, I realized my unforgiving heart was eating me alive. Every time I would see these women (which was daily), I would feel the pain again. Every time I pulled out the emails, I was reliving their cruel words against me. They had moved on and forgotten about it, but I was still anchored in the pain. I knew I had to get freedom.

Jesus said I am to love my neighbor, which can be hard enough. But then He took it to a whole new level. Actually, to a whole different stratosphere: "You have heard that it was said, 'Love your neighbor and hate your enemy.' But I tell you, love your enemies and pray for those who persecute you" (Matthew 5:43–44 NIV).

Whoa! The "love your neighbor" thing is already master's degree material. It will take me a lifetime to get a handle on that. Yet Jesus is saying it goes beyond my neighbor. I am to love my enemies.

When Jesus spoke these words, He was likely talking about real enemies. In the crowd were people who had been in battle against other nations. There were probably people who had family members the Romans had killed or imprisoned. There were families who had their life savings stolen by tax collectors.

Think about the story we just looked at in a previous chapter: the Good Samaritan. Jesus told the story to answer the question, "Who is my neighbor?" And so, our neighbor is the next person we meet. We are to love our neighbor. But Jesus specifically uses an enemy of the Jewish people to further His point.

You are not only to love your neighbor. You are to love your enemy—the person who has wronged you. Perhaps it was as benign as cutting you off in traffic or knocking over your mailbox or being loud and obnoxious at the last parent/teacher assembly. Every day, we face people we wish didn't exist, or at least didn't exist in our presence. Those are the very people we are called to love.

One day, Jesus was talking to His disciples. He had just selected the twelve to be His closest disciples, and He began teaching them on the hillside. Although hundreds were standing around listening, Luke tells us that Jesus was specifically teaching His disciples. His words are as relevant today as they were on that day two thousand years ago:

> "Love your enemies. Let them bring out the best in you, not the worst. When someone gives you a hard time, respond with the energies of prayer for that person. If someone slaps you in the face, stand there and take it. If someone grabs your shirt, giftwrap your best coat and make a present of it. If someone takes unfair advantage of you, use the occasion to practice the servant life. No more tit-for-tat stuff. Live generously.
> "Here is a simple rule of thumb for behavior: Ask

yourself what you want people to do for you; then grab the initiative and do it for them! If you only love the lovable, do you expect a pat on the back? Run-of-the-mill sinners do that. If you only help those who help you, do you expect a medal? Garden-variety sinners do that. If you only give for what you hope to get out of it, do you think that's charity? The stingiest of pawnbrokers does that.

"I tell you, love your enemies. Help and give without expecting a return. You'll never—I promise—regret it. Live out this God-created identity the way our Father lives toward us, generously and graciously, even when we're at our worst. Our Father is kind; you be kind."

LUKE 6:27–36 MSG

Do you see how this kind of behavior could change the world ? What would happen if every person who claims to follow Jesus actually followed this teaching? What if, for the rest of your life, you didn't worry about anything else in the Bible except for these three paragraphs? And what if every person who claims to be a Christian did the same thing?

Our politics would be different.

Our schoolrooms would be different.

Our church board meetings would be different.

Our playgrounds would be different.

Our televised debates would be different.

Our songs and TV shows and movies would be different.

Our family reunions would be different.

Our tweets would be different.

Our news media would be different.

Our highways and streets and neighborhoods would be safer.

Let's face it. My life would be different, and so would yours. Loving and forgiving those who have wronged you is a game changer. The culture couldn't help but sit up and take notice, simply because it is so rare.

Let's rewrite one of those verses above and use some analogies we can all identify with:

- When your neighbor drives through your grass, do something tangible to make his lawn look nicer.

- When a friend gossips about you and says things that are neither nice nor accurate, do what you can to build them up in the eyes of others.

- When a teacher singles you out and makes life twice as tough on you as the rest of the students, make him some cookies or send him a note thanking him for his service.

- When your wife leaves you for another man and you want nothing more than to punch him in the face and cause both of them just half the pain they have caused you, resist. Pray. Ask God for the strength to forgive. Find a way to tangibly love them.

I know what you're thinking. *Forgiveness doesn't make the pain go away. It doesn't make what they did to me right. It doesn't mean they didn't cause irreparable damage.*

There is a big difference between forgiving and trusting.

If your son takes your car, drives recklessly, and damages it, you might instantly grant him forgiveness. But it might be a long time before he gets the car keys again. You have forgiven him, but he has to rebuild the trust.

If you have been in an abusive relationship, there might come a time when the abuser has a change of heart and asks you to forgive him. The Bible says we are to forgive instantly and completely, because God forgave us so completely for our sins.

But trust is a different issue. Trust must be rebuilt slowly. Forgiveness is based on grace, but trust is based on behavior. There is no way to earn forgiveness. Yet trust must be earned.

You should forgive your abuser instantly and completely. But you should not let him back into your house. You should think twice before you drop the restraining order. You should consider the consequences before you allow your kids around him. Drawing appropriate boundaries doesn't mean you haven't forgiven. It only means you are making room for trust to be rebuilt.

But forgiveness is required, and it is necessary. If we are marked by His love, then we will forgive when we've been hurt, and that forgiveness will look different from one person to the next.

An old proverb says it this way: "If your enemy is hungry, give him food to eat; if he is thirsty, give him water to drink. In doing this, you will heap burning coals on his head, and the LORD will reward you" (Proverbs 25:21–22 NIV).

You've heard the axiom "Kill them with kindness." That comes from this verse! (Well actually, it doesn't come from this verse. It was first said in the 1500s and related to apes that would kill their young by hugging them to death. Literally. But, dead baby apes aside, it's still a cool phrase and has a direct correlation to this passage.)

Now you might be thinking, *That's right. I'd love to heap burning coals on his head! And then I'll stand and watch the skin burn off his bones.* I have two thoughts for you: (a) you might be watching too much of *The Walking Dead*, and (b) this suggests you haven't yet completely forgiven him.

I think Solomon is encouraging you to do something tangible for your enemy. Don't just think nice thoughts, but actually do something to bless that person. Take action. Let God be the one to turn your kindness into conviction (a.k.a. *coals*) in that person's heart. You just focus on being loving.

The women who went on a gossip rampage about me had said they were sorry nearly a year before. But I hadn't completely forgiven. I continued to rehearse the pain in my mind over and over, nursing it like a wounded animal, when I really needed to release it.

God got my attention one day as I read over the emails once again, this time asking Him to help me let it go. In my hands were the printed emails, by then wrinkled and worn from constant use. He prompted me to destroy them. I protested, "But I might need them for proof someday."

Proof of what? That I hadn't truly forgiven them? I ripped the pages into shreds. I went to my computer and permanently deleted the emails from my archives. They were gone. No longer could I live in the past.

I can't describe the freedom I felt in that moment. It was as though my heart had been 80 percent blocked and I just had open-heart surgery. I could breathe again. I no longer felt the weight. In the days and weeks to come, I noticed that the pain I had felt around those coworkers started to subside. God was healing me.

I started looking for ways to love them. My wife and I bought flowers for one of the women on her next birthday; we took another and her husband out to eat and let them both know how grateful we were for their friendship. It took time, but the relationships were slowly rebuilt.

Those who are marked by love are different in the way they forgive. They are different in the way they love. They are different in how they act toward people they don't like or who have done them wrong.

Don't follow my example. I waited a full year to love like Jesus.

Follow the example of Jesus. On the day of His crucifixion, as He's hanging on the cross, broken and bruised, His face unrecognizable, He utters these words about His executioners:

> *"Father, forgive them, for they do not know what they are doing."*
>
> LUKE 23:34 NIV

19
IT'S A FACT

We're moved when we hear stories of forgiveness or unexpected love. You may have cried tears of disbelief when you read Madge Rodda's story of forgiveness in the previous chapter. Perhaps you sat and contemplated how Gene Ort could have such a selfless focus after losing his daughter.

But this isn't just a warm and fuzzy dream of impacting the world through our acts of love. It's actually already making a difference, both in your health and in the world at large. There is scientific proof that people who are marked by love are healthier and happier.

Here are some facts:

Fact 1: Love is the key to happiness. In 1939, Harvard University began a study to track the physical and emotional well-being of men. The focus was on two study samples: men who grew up poor and men who graduated from Harvard. The men were studied for seventy-five years, which took multiple generations of researchers. The researchers studied blood samples, conducted brain scans, issued surveys, and interviewed these men over the span of their lifetimes.

Guess what the study revealed? It wasn't money, status,

prestige, or assets that determined happiness. Rather, it concluded, "The biggest predictor of your happiness and fulfillment overall in life is, basically, love."[26]

Melanie Curtin, a journalist with Inc.com, summed up the research this way:

> *The data is clear that, in the end, you could have all the money you've ever wanted, a successful career, and be in good physical health, but without loving relationships, you won't be happy.*
>
> *The next time you're scrolling through Facebook instead of being present at the table with your significant other, or you're considering staying late at the office instead of getting together with your close friend, or you catch yourself working on a Saturday instead of going to the farmer's market with your sister, consider making a different choice.*

That's some good advice.

Fact 2: Love is the key to health. It's pretty much universal that we all want to be healthy. No one wishes for poor health. Here is what I suggest to increase your odds of good health: *Become a more loving person.*

Carnegie Mellon University issued a landmark paper in 2004 based on years of research. The research found that "people who are happy, lively, calm, or exhibit other positive emotions are less likely to become ill when they are exposed to a cold virus than those who report few of these emotions."[27] This is about positive choices—like assuming the best in others, learning to forgive, and not holding grudges. In general, becoming a more loving person will strengthen your immunity.

The Ohio State University Medical Center conducted

another study in which married couples were given blister wounds. (I'm not sure how the people were given blisters, or who in their right mind would sign up, but I digress.) The wounds healed nearly twice as fast in people who expressed love toward their spouses as compared with those who were hostile toward each other.[28]

Fact 3: Forgiveness can improve mental health. Scientific studies have proven that choosing to forgive (i.e., love) those who have harmed us in some way improves our mental health. Research has shown that "forgiveness is linked to mental health outcomes such as reduced anxiety, depression and major psychiatric disorders, as well as with fewer physical health symptoms and lower mortality rates."[29]

Fact 4: Loving others during national disasters is making a difference. When we choose to love others suffering from the effects of a hurricane, wildfire, earthquake, or other disaster, we are being the hands and feet of Jesus. A recent report in *USA Today* concluded that "faith-based organizations are integral partners in state and federal disaster relief efforts."[30] The director of the Department of Homeland Security's Center for Faith-Based & Neighborhood Partnerships said, "FEMA cannot do what it does so well without the cooperation of faith-based non-profit organizations and churches."

Fact 5: Being generous is directly linked to happiness. Most of us believe that a significant determinant of our own happiness is whether we feel loved and cared for. And yet some studies have shown that it is not how much people love us, but how much we show love to others, that determines our happiness. In a recent study, "participants were either given $5 or $20 as part of an experiment. Participants in both groups were then asked to either spend the money on themselves or on others. Those who spent the money on others, it turned out, grew happier than those who spent it on themselves."[31]

The author of the study concluded, "When you are generous, the story you tell yourself is that you have everything you need and more, which is why you can afford to be generous. In contrast, when you are miserly and greedy with your affection, the story you tell yourself is that you are a beggar who is dissatisfied with what you have and that you need more to be happy."

Fact 6: Proverbs agrees. Perhaps you can find fault in these scientific studies and research conclusions. But I find it interesting that each study backs up what the writers of these Proverbs concluded thousands of years ago:

- "A cheerful disposition is good for your health; gloom and doom leave you bone-tired" (Proverbs 17:22 MSG).
- "Gracious words are a honeycomb, sweet to the soul and healing to the bones" (Proverbs 16:24 NIV).
- "A peaceful heart leads to a healthy body; jealousy is like cancer in the bones" (Proverbs 14:30 NLT).

Sometimes it's a scientific study that persuades us to be more loving. Other times it's looking in the mirror at our own lack of love that wakes us up. That's what happened to me on a hot summer day in Indiana.

20
THE DAY A PUNK TAUGHT
ME ABOUT LOVE

It was a Saturday, and one of my goals was to stay home all day, but just after lunch I had to run down to the corner nursery to pick up fertilizer. On my way home, I stopped for gas when I noticed something very strange. In the gas station parking lot, there was a car pointed at a forty-five-degree angle downward with its back wheels in the air. The driver had tried to jump a curb, not realizing there was an eighteen-inch drop-off between the gas station parking lot and the lot next door. His car was perched on the curb, and he was in deep trouble. I said the first thing that came to my mind: "Oh my! Sucks to be you."

I watched for a few minutes as two guys circled the car, considering their options. I was going to drive home but needed gas anyway, so I pulled over to a pump where I could lurk and watch this scene from behind my car.

The two were about twenty years old, and they both had multiple piercings and full-body tattoos. I just stared from the safety of my outpost behind the gas pump, amazed, wondering what these idiots were thinking when they tried to jump the curb.

Then I noticed the car. It was a newer-model luxury vehicle—easily worth $80,000. As I thought about that, I became even more judgmental, thinking, *These punks are driving around in Daddy's car and just messed it up.* I even said to the guy pumping gas next to me, who had walked over closer to the crisis and just returned, "A couple punks messed up Daddy's car, huh?"

That's when I began to realize how wrong I was. He replied, "Nope. There are three little kids still in the car, and their dad was driving." I looked past the "punks" and saw a young man and his wife, both very shaken, trying to figure out what to do.

These young "punks" had stopped their car to help a family in distress. I'm ashamed to say that stopping to help them had never crossed my mind. *It was my day off. I was working in my yard. I was busy.* Plus, my judgmental thoughts toward the jerks who had gotten themselves into this position consumed me. Besides, what could I do? They needed major help, like a crane or a tow truck.

As I finished pumping my gas, one of the "punks" saw me lurking and called out, "Hey, can you give us a hand?" They had analyzed the situation and figured that four or five men could lift the car off the curb and get this guy on his way. I would never have attempted that or even thought it was possible. But within about ten minutes, four of us (through the very capable leadership of the "punks") got the young family on their way. The driver quickly grabbed his wallet and offered to pay the young men, but they waved him off, got back in their car, and drove away. They didn't want money or recognition. They wanted to help.

I got back in my car. I should have felt good about helping the helpless, but instead I drove home feeling guilty for how quick I had been to judge. Rather than being happy about the rescue, I was painfully aware that I would have just watched from behind my car if the "punk" hadn't called out.

My judgment came from a deep-seated stereotype. I wasn't judging these guys because of anything they had said or done. I'd never met them. My judgment came because of a preconceived idea of how guys that age, with those clothes and those tattoos and piercings, would typically act. And in a nanosecond, I condemned them. *They are no-good, entitled slackers who just ran straight into some serious consequences*, I thought. *Serves them right!*

Stereotypes are subtle. Sometimes we don't even know we have them. *Merriam-Webster* defines a *stereotype* this way: "To believe unfairly that all people or things with a particular characteristic are the same."[32]

Another way to think about a stereotype is as a *generalization*, which is defined as: "A statement about a group of people or things that is based on only a few people or things in that group."[33]

A generalization might be as simple as sending out a negative tweet after having a bad meal at a restaurant. You are aware that your friend also got sick after eating at that establishment, so you confidently put it out on Twitter: "Don't eat at _____. Everyone is getting sick."

The most common stereotypes or generalizations are related to race. In your town, it might be a statistical fact that most violent crimes are committed by purple people. This is reinforced as you watch the local news each night and hear more reports of violent crimes—and most of them involve purple people. So you subconsciously form a stereotype within you toward purple people. *I must protect my family and my way of life by staying away from purple people*, you would think, *and if I'm near them, I don't want to tick them off.*

The actual facts may suggest that 98 percent of the purple people in your community are law-abiding, peaceful individuals who, just like you, desire to raise their kids in a good environment. But your belief, while rooted in some actual facts, won't let you see the bigger picture.

John Piper says a generalization turns to racism...

> ...when you treat all the members of a group as if all must be characterized by a negative generalization. Or when you speak disparagingly of an entire group on the basis of a negative generalization without any regard for those in the group who don't fit the generalization.[34]

Your generalizations become prejudice when they lead you to act in less than loving ways toward people of different ethnicities. When you treat people as beneath you, or not as good as you, because they belong to a type or category of people who are not like you, that is racism or discrimination. And Jesus stands against both.

Most of us don't think of ourselves as racist. And maybe we aren't. But I think it's likely that all of us have blind spots that cause us to make unloving statements or assumptions about certain categories of people. Here are a few to consider:

Immigrant-ist: You have no problems with foreigners, but you wear a shirt that says, "Welcome to America! Now speak English!" You are very concerned that *those* people don't come into your country and mess with your way of life.

Midwestern-ist: You think people who live in the midwestern part of the country are gun-toting, uneducated farmers who keep getting in the way of progress.

Coast-ist: You assume those who live on the left coast or right coast are fat-cat liberals who want our country to become socialist.

Rich-ist: You look down on rich people: *They act entitled,* you think. *They probably inherited their money. They don't have any problems.*

Poor-ist: You make generalized statements about poor people. "They must be lazy," you say. "They are living off welfare even though they can work."

NASCAR-ist: You are pretty sure people who watch NASCAR are toothless hicks who would spit tobacco juice on your shoe if you got close enough.

Fat-ist: You assume overweight people can stop overeating anytime they want—they are just undisciplined.

LGBT-ist: You are convinced the gay and lesbian agenda is being heralded by perverted, sex-obsessed people who are trying to push their agenda on our Christian nation.

Democrat-ist: You are confident Democrats don't love America and only want someone else to pay their way.

Republican-ist: You think Republicans are all rich

bigots who only want more money and care nothing for the poor.

Christian-ist: You think people who rely on religion for a crutch are weak.

The list could be much longer, but you get the idea. My guess is that one or more of these pricked your conscience, because you know you've been guilty. I know I have.

In your local community, you may unfairly categorize people based on where they live or where they send their kids to school. Or you may judge those who go away to college instead of staying home and working. Or you may stereotype people who attend a certain church.

Here is what Jesus had to say about treating people poorly based on how they are different from us: "Stop judging by mere appearances, but instead judge correctly" (John 7:24 NIV).

Paul said it this way when he wrote to the church in Galatia:

> *In Christ's family there can be no division into*
> *Jew and non-Jew, slave and free, male and female.*
> *Among us you are all equal. That is, we are all in a*
> *common relationship with Jesus Christ.*
> GALATIANS 3:28 MSG

If Paul had written this in the twenty-first century, he might have said it like this:

> *Followers of Jesus can't treat people differently, or*
> *think in terms of the blacks and the whites, the*
> *Americans and the immigrants, the rich and the poor,*
> *the gay and the straight, or even as men and women.*

In the family of Jesus, you are all equal. We all have the same rights to a relationship with God.

And yet our pride drives us to compare. Pride is so subtle. It twists its way into our hearts and makes us less than Jesus-like. Every now and then, we hear ourselves talking or consider our thoughts, and we're terrified at how much we think of ourselves as better than others.

If we are going to be followers of Christ who are marked by the love of God, then we must get a handle on our stereotypes. You see, a person who is marked by love does not compare in order to make himself feel better, and he doesn't speak negatively about any group of people.

A person who is marked by love looks for ways to serve others and will stand against racism or stereotypes. A person who is marked by love is convinced to her core that Jesus died because of His love for all and that each human being is as precious in His eyes as the next.

I'm sure I can't sum up this chapter any better than Jesus did as He finished up the Sermon on the Mount:

> *"Don't pick on people, jump on their failures, criticize their faults—unless, of course, you want the same treatment. That critical spirit has a way of boomeranging. It's easy to see a smudge on your neighbor's face and be oblivious to the ugly sneer on your own. Do you have the nerve to say, 'Let me wash your face for you,' when your own face is distorted by contempt? It's this whole traveling road-show mentality all over again, playing a holier-than-thou part instead of just living your part. Wipe that ugly sneer off your own face, and you might be fit to offer a washcloth to your neighbor. . . .*

Here is a simple, rule-of-thumb guide for behavior:
Ask yourself what you want people to do for you, then
grab the initiative and do it for them. Add up God's
Law and Prophets and this is what you get."

MATTHEW 7:1–5, 12 MSG

That's it. It's just that simple.

21
PEOPLE DON'T CARE HOW MUCH YOU KNOW

A Modern-Day Parable:

> *Ever since he was a little boy, Thomas Giovante had an interest in the Democratic Republic of Congo in central Africa. When he was about twelve years old, he read a story in* National Geographic *about the children of Congo, and it stayed with him for years. He talked to his parents and friends about it and said, "Someday, I'm going to Congo to help!" They loved his passion and encouraged him to pursue his dreams.*
>
> *However, by the time Thomas graduated from high school, he was focused on sports, medicine, friends, and fun, and he mostly forgot about the story that marked him so clearly as a child. He started into college and began pursuing a degree in physical therapy with a minor in business, but he felt empty inside—as if nothing he was doing was worth anything. He watched his parents in the rat race of life making money, spending money, making more money, spending more money—and never having*

enough. He didn't want that. No, he knew there had to be something more.

By the time he was a junior at the university, Thomas began to attend a weekly Bible study on campus. He was not even sure why he went the first time, except he had a gnawing void inside that didn't seem to go away, regardless of how many girls he met or frat parties he attended. A friend had kept nagging him to go, so one day when he was wallowing in a depressed state of despair, he finally gave in. To his surprise, he somewhat liked it. Parts of it were weird, and there were some geeks there, with whom he for sure did not want to be seen, but there were also some cool people he knew—and a great talk about some of the stuff that was going on inside of him that he had never told anyone.

Through the rest of his junior year, this gathering became a regular part of Thomas's week. He was feeling a new sense of hope and direction for his life. God was doing something deep in his heart, and although he didn't fully understand it, he knew it was marking him for the rest of his life.

At one of the gatherings just before the semester ended, a woman spoke on the plight of the children in the world who were facing poverty and malnutrition. In a nanosecond, all the memories from the National Geographic *story he had read as a child about the Republic of Congo came rushing back into Thomas's mind like a huge ocean wave. As though he had just read the story for the first time, he instantly experienced again all the feelings he had for the people of Congo and the desire to go there and help! Except this time, his dream was infused with a desire to help them spiritually!*

Within two months, he dropped out of school,
enrolled in a summer training program for short-
term missionaries, and began raising support to begin
his term in Congo that fall. His friends and family
quickly noticed his passion and desire to help the
people of Congo, so it didn't take long at all to raise
the support he needed. By September, he was standing
in a village about two hundred kilometers north
of Kinshasa, at the western edge of the Republic of
Congo. His childhood dream was finally coming true.

Through the training he had received over the
summer, his passion was stronger than ever to let
the people of Congo know how much they matter to
God. He wanted them to experience the life-changing
grace of Christ that had changed him just a short
time ago. He knew that so many of them were dying
each day; there wasn't much time to deliver the good
news of eternal life!

He quickly established himself, found a place
to live, and started preparing for his first public
services. The people of the village watched with
curiosity—a foreign man living in their village,
eating their food, setting up a tent. It was all very
strange, but they watched with huge anticipation.
Maybe this was the answer. Maybe he was here
to offer them the help for which they longed. They
had heard of white men in other villages bringing
medicine and food and supplies. But up until now,
it had been largely a fantasy for them. And so, their
children continued to die, and their young men
continued to turn to fighting and violence. When
people got sick, they rarely recovered.

Thomas found an interpreter who knew both
English and the native language, Lingala, and he

began making plans for his first public service when he could tell the village residents about Jesus.

It was interesting to Thomas how other missionaries in surrounding villages weren't preaching the good news at all. They had teamed up with UNICEF and other organizations, and they were busy providing food and medicine. Thomas thought that was a worthy effort but wondered why they had abandoned their first calling to deliver the good news of Jesus Christ.

The week finally came when Thomas held his first public meeting. He could see the smiles on the people's faces all week as he handed out flyers inviting them to the first public service. The anticipation was building. He was even second-guessing whether he had brought over a large enough tent from the States and whether the public-address system that was purchased for him would be loud enough for the crowd that was sure to gather.

On the first Sunday morning, hundreds gathered for the opening service, spilling out all sides of the tent. Thomas had found a village musician to play songs as people gathered, and that seemed to raise the excitement level even more. When the time came, Thomas stood up to deliver his very first message to the people of this small village in Congo, and it was a great message. A little rough through a translator, but he still felt it was one of his best deliveries ever. He laid out the Gospel presentation in the clearest way he possibly could. He was certain some people would respond.

Massive disappointment.

That is the only way to describe how Thomas felt following that service and in the weeks to *come. The crowd that started as several hundred dwindled quickly to less than twenty. The smiles and anticipation that seemed to be all around during his first few weeks in the village turned back to hollow faces filled with desperation. The wailing of adults and children alike every time another villager succumbed to hunger or disease seemed to get louder in Thomas's ears every day.*

The dream of Thomas Giovante seemed to die a little more every day. No matter how much he tried or how loud he talked, he couldn't seem to bridge the gap between the hearts of the people and the eternal life that was waiting for them in heaven. If they only understood, if they only would listen, it would change their perspectives and mark their destinies. But they didn't understand, and they wouldn't listen. And so, the dream of Thomas Giovante to make a difference in Congo remained a dream.

Within six months, he packed up and headed back home, his head hanging in frustration and shame.

Thomas Giovante had failed. His heart was in the right place. He had great intentions. His motives were pure. But he failed to accomplish his goal of converting the people of Congo to Christianity.

Why did Thomas fail? Why did he not get the results he so badly wanted? What did he do wrong? Maybe he gave up too soon. If he had just kept at it, eventually he would have started to see results.

Maybe, but I don't believe so. I believe the reason Thomas failed is that he ignored a classic axiom, first said by Teddy Roosevelt:

People don't care how much you know until they know how much you care.[35]

Thomas did what churches in America have been doing for decades. He did what many pastors have been trained to do. He did what thousands of frustrated preachers do every Sunday morning. He just stood up and preached the Good News of a God who loves the whole world, but his listeners didn't feel that love. With great intellect and theological accuracy, he talked to the people about eternal life with Jesus in heaven, but he didn't give them an experience of who Jesus is and why they would want to be with Him forever. He told them God is love and cares for every one of them, but they didn't feel loved or cared for. He told them stories *about* Jesus, but he didn't introduce them *to* Jesus.

The people of the village came to the tent after listening to the cries of their hungry children all night long. On their way to Thomas's services, they walked past the hut filled wall-to-wall with mats of dying AIDS and malaria patients—most of whom they knew and loved. They walked to the tent with the recent memory of a child who died of diarrhea and the reports of their adolescent sons dying on the front lines of a bloody revolution. Those were the people, the issues, and the problems on their minds.

And so, when Thomas Giovante talked of a Jesus who cared, they didn't feel it. When he talked of a God who so loved the world, they never experienced that love. In fact, truthfully, the more Thomas talked, the angrier they became. They wondered what type of God would allow the devastation surrounding them. Once again, their hopes were dashed. Starvation and sadness were the only roads ahead for them.

Thomas did what many of us do in our daily interactions with people around us. We invite them to church, tell them we are praying for them, "evangelize" them, and point them to Bible verses we think will address their current crisis. But we do little to let them know we really care.

Do a little exercise with me. This won't take long, so just play along. When I say, "go," hold both your hands in front of your eyes, not much further out than the end of your nose. Keep your eyes open and hold your hands there for about five seconds. Ready? Okay, go!

Waiting.

Okay, what did you see? Not much, right? Your hands were covering most of your view. Perhaps you could see a little peripherally or between your hands or through your fingers, but for the most part your vision was blocked.

When people lack food or basic medical attention for someone they love, those problems become just like your hands in front of your eyes. It is all they can see. It doesn't matter how eloquently or convincingly you explain to them that God cares, their problems keep them from seeing that truth. All they can see are the problems right in front of their eyes, and the more you talk about how God cares about their problems, the more clueless they think you are. And sometimes, they get angry at this God you speak of who doesn't really seem to care about them.

Unless you help people with the problems right in front of their eyes, most will not hear you. Unless you begin to offer assistance to the sick, food for the hungry, and education for those who need it, you won't have earned the right to be heard.

But when you set up the clinics, bring in the food, and start offering vocational training, you earn that right. People will then be willing to hear that God loves them, because they see you meeting their needs. Through your actions, they will feel the hand of a Savior who cares, and they will want to know more. You will have helped move their hands away from their faces, and the farther away those hands move, the more they can clearly see the smiling face of Jesus in you.

Here is the truth: many people around you haven't had the same experience with Jesus as you. They have a handful of problems right in front of their eyes, and for them, those problems seem as huge, overwhelming, and serious as if they were living in the Republic of Congo. If we want to help people take steps in their faith, we first have to recognize and address the problems directly in front of them.

The reason many people want nothing to do with your God is because He seems irrelevant to their lives. They can't even consider their spiritual selves, because they have other looming worries. They need help. They have real problems and real issues.

There is a man who is on his second marriage, but it is falling apart just like the first one. And he thinks he'll go crazy if he cannot figure out how to make this one work.

There is a single mom who desperately needs help. Her kids totally run her life, and it is nonstop stress from morning until night. She yells at them all the time, and she's sure they would be better off without her.

There is an older woman who has chronic pain, and she would honestly rather be dead. She has been lonely since her husband died, her kids are too busy to spend any time with her, and she has begun to rely too much on the pain pills her doctor prescribed.

There is a sixteen-year-old boy whose uncle has been sexually molesting him for two years. He figures it is his own fault and that something must be wrong with him, and he has been experimenting with whatever he can find to dull the pain.

There is a middle-aged couple with two teenage daughters. They found out one just became pregnant, and they suspect the other one is addicted to drugs and alcohol. They thought they were good parents, but now they aren't so sure. They are mortified that their friends might find out, and the distance and tension between them and their daughters continues to grow.

There is a young couple with small children who have been funding their lifestyle with credit cards for years now. He just lost his job, and she is working extra hours to try to make up the difference. However, the interest payments alone are killing them financially. It is stressing their marriage, and they are taking their anger out on their kids. They are just about to lose the house and both cars, and they have no idea where they will go if that happens.

There is a lesbian couple who both grew up in the church and continue to have a strong life of faith. They were recently married and are building a life together. They long for a community where they can study the Bible and hang out with others who are spiritually like-minded. But every time they try to connect to a church, they are rejected and asked to worship somewhere else. They are just about done with church.

There is a woman who has been yelled at, beaten up, and sexually abused her entire life. Men only want her for one thing. Once they get it, they discard her like an old newspaper. She accepted a new job working for a Christian, which she was so excited about, but now even that guy is starting to hit on her. Her hatred for God is growing exponentially by the day.

Do you see? Men and women and teenagers and children and elderly folks in your community have problems right in front of their eyes, problems so big they can't see anything else. You work with them, go to school with them, sit by them at church, and live next door to them. They are dealing with the consequences of their own regretful choices or the damaging actions of others. They have gone through a huge crisis, such as the loss of a child or lifelong mate. They are plodding through life with little or no purpose.

This is where we can make a real difference. When you are marked by love, you can't help but reach out to others with compassion and love. Sometimes that means stopping long enough to listen. Other times it means preparing a meal or meeting a physical need. Stop reciting Bible verses long enough to look into someone's eyes and let them know you really care, that you will be there for them, that they will get through this, and that you won't leave them until they do.

It's true. People don't care how much you know until they know how much you care.

22
THERE'S MORE TO LIFE
THAN GREEN GRASS

When we left Indiana and moved to Texas, one of the things I missed the most was my John Deere tractor. I *loved* my John Deere. But more than that, I loved mowing my grass. Some would say I was a little bit perfectionistic about having a perfectly manicured lawn. A friend once asked me if I snapped a chalk-line before I mowed so my lines would be straight. He was mocking me, but I took it as a compliment.

We had a little house on an acre and a half, and spending time in my yard was therapy for me. For two hours, I would hear nothing but the drone of the tractor and get lost in my own thoughts. I would brainstorm solutions for problems at work, I would dream about the future, and I would reflect on the people most important to me.

And I would think about the jerk who lived next door.

I really didn't know Tom that well. We each had four kids, and they all went to the same schools. Tom worked for the utility company and was really a nice guy. But evidently no one had taught him how to water his grass. I had thoroughly researched the type of grass in our lawns and our local climate conditions, and I knew that you should water thoroughly in the morning three or four times a week. Give it a chance to soak in and then dry out, and the grass roots will go deep toward the water, creating a much healthier turf.

Not Tom. He would water his grass all day, every day. That's not an exaggeration—he ran three-hour cycles, and he did it three times a day. How do I know this? Because I snuck into his garage one time while he was gone and looked at his irrigation timer. He literally watered his grass nine hours every day.

I shouldn't have cared, except our lawns bordered each other, and my yard was downhill from his. His water runoff would flood my grass every day. It was hard to keep it growing because it never dried out. If I tried mowing that section, I'd leave muddy, rutted tracks.

I can fix this, I naively thought. *Once Tom understands the error of his way, he'll change his sprinkler settings and my yard will stop flooding.*

No such luck. Tom and I had a short conversation, and he set me straight: "My lawn guy set this up, and I'm not changing it."

I let it go for a few weeks, but every time I mowed, I would get to that side of the lawn and my blood would start boiling. I was thinking some not-very-nice thoughts about Tom.

I learned that Purdue University had a turf science department, so I printed off some of their documents and took them over to Tom. I thought he'd appreciate knowing that his lawn guy was wrong. The next day, I noticed his sprinklers were still running nine hours a day. And the day after that. And the next week. Nothing changed.

Then one day while I was on my John Deere stewing about the idiot next door, it hit me: *It isn't Tom who needs to change. It's me.*

What was so wrong with my heart that I would allow

this anger and hatred to grow over how much a guy waters his lawn? He wasn't doing this to hurt me. He was just living his life. He wasn't doing anything unkind or illegal or unethical. Yet I was building him into a monster in my own mind because he was messing up my perfect little lawn.

Perhaps you have experienced a similar situation. Have you considered what makes us respond in unloving ways? Why do we so quickly assume that another person is an idiot or a jerk—or whatever term we choose?

I'd like to suggest three things you can do to help you become a more loving person:

1. Create space in your life. I live in the fourth largest American city with 6.7 million of my closest friends, and traffic has become a regular part of my life. My office commute typically takes about an hour. And it's not a laid back hour either. It's a fast-moving, high-paced, lane-changing, horn-honking, stop-and-go, heart-racing hour. And it's not unusual for me to yell "Idiot!" at a driver who cuts me off or drives too slow in *my* lane.

How I respond to others while I'm going seventy miles per hour in traffic may be the clearest regular indication that I have not yet mastered being marked by love. If I'm ever self-deceived enough to think I am the poster child for what a loving human looks like, I need to consider the inner dialogue and, I'll be honest, occasional *verbal* outbursts that happen when I'm in a hurry to get somewhere.

The solution? Margin. Space. Room to breathe.

When I've only allowed myself forty-five minutes for a forty-five-minute drive, I'm going to be on edge. I'm going to be irritable. I'm going to get mad at the people who get in my way. But if I leave seventy-five minutes before I need to arrive, then suddenly I'm more patient, more caring, and more tolerant of the people around me.

In his book *Margin: Restoring Emotional, Physical, Financial, and Time Reserves to Overloaded Lives*, Richard Swenson, MD, describes margin like this:

> *Margin is the space between our load and our limits. It is the amount allowed beyond that which is needed. It is something held in reserve for contingencies or unanticipated situations. Margin is the gap between rest and exhaustion, the space between breathing freely and suffocating.*[36]

Everything in our culture tells us to ignore margins. Spend more money than you make. Work longer and harder. Drive faster. Do more. Be more. Buy more.

But when we don't intentionally leave space in our lives, we become individuals who are not very loving. Why? Because loving others takes time.

When you've filled your schedule from the time you get up until you go to bed, you don't have time for the people you meet throughout the day who need a listening ear or an encouraging word.

When your outgo is bigger than your income, you have no room in your budget to respond to people in need.

Margin makes you pleasant. No margin makes you grumpy. Margin allows you to be generous. No margin makes you Scrooge-like. Margin helps you listen. Without margin, you come across as someone who doesn't care.

I like what Kary Oberbrunner wrote about margin on his blog, *Igniting Souls*:

Margins Create Space for. . .

1. *Laughter:* You can't laugh if everything is serious.
2. *Generosity:* You can't give if you have nothing left.
3. *Memories:* You can't remember if you weren't present.
4. *Prayer:* You can't pray if you're self-sufficient.
5. *Dreams:* You can't dream if you can't imagine.
6. *Love:* You can't love if you're self-absorbed.
7. *Exercise:* You can't exercise if you don't value yourself.
8. *Creativity:* You can't create if you're merely a machine.
9. *Experimentation:* You can't experiment if you don't have time to fail.
10. *Reflection:* You can't reflect if you don't value rest.
11. *Spontaneity:* You can't be in the moment if you're stuck in the future.
12. *Rest:* You can't sit if you can't stop.
13. *Joy:* You can't pour out if you haven't been filled up.
14. *Peace:* You can't breathe deeply if you can't catch your breath.
15. *Friendships:* You can't expect to have friends if you fail to be one.[37]

When I live on less than I make, I have the financial margin that keeps an unexpected expense from capsizing me. That way, I can respond in the moment to someone else's real need. When I leave space in my schedule, I have time to stop and listen to someone who needs an ear or time to jump in and help a neighbor pick up his car from the mechanic. I will be sensitive enough to notice someone around me who is obviously hurting.

I saw this happen in real life a few years back when I was

eating at a restaurant in Miami. We had chosen to be seated outside in front of the restaurant on the patio, close to the sidewalk. I watched a guy come in off the street and approach each table, one by one. He was obviously looking for money, so I assumed he was homeless.

At each table, he was quickly turned away. People just wanted to eat their meals without being disturbed. I could see patrons looking around for the restaurant staff, hoping someone would tell this man to go away.

That is, until he approached the table next to us. I had noticed these two gentlemen. They were having some type of business discussion. It looked serious to me. But at the arrival of Homeless Harry, they instantly gave this vagrant their full attention. I'm guessing he asked for money, but it was the response of the man at the table that still sticks with me all these years later: "I might be able to help you. But I'd love to hear your story first."

And he listened patiently, asking questions and seeking to understand. He didn't condemn. He didn't shoo him away. He didn't demean him. He treated this man with dignity. He intently listened to his story and expressed compassion. And then he gave him a twenty-dollar bill.

Homeless Harry walked away after that, and the restaurant patron returned to his business conversation without missing a beat. I could tell he wasn't trying to impress anyone. This is just who he was. Margin was a way of life for him. On that day, he had space for the person who came across his path. And he had a $20 bill in his pocket available to meet a need.

I have so much to learn.

2. Remove the things that make you unloving. A verse in Philippians offers some great advice:

> *Whatever is true, whatever is noble, whatever
> is right, whatever is pure, whatever is lovely,
> whatever is admirable—if anything is excellent or
> praiseworthy—think about such things.*
>
> PHILIPPIANS 4:8 NIV

I think the opposite is also true. Perhaps it might be written this way:

> *Whatever pulls you down, whatever makes you less
> loving, whatever is a negative drain to your life,
> whatever takes you to an unhealthy place—if there
> is anything that makes you marked by negativity
> instead of love—remove those things from your life.*

Let me make this incredibly tangible. On November 7, 2012, I stopped watching cable news. That might not seem like a big deal to most people, but I was a news junkie. For years, I probably averaged seven to ten hours of news-watching a week. I *loved* watching the news, hearing different angles on the news, and listening to incredibly smart commentators share their opinion about the news.

I would increase my intake of cable news during the election season. I loved watching every debate and then hearing the debates about the debates. For me, politics was a game and I was spectator number one. But that all changed on the eve of the 2012 election, when I turned it off, cold turkey. I was done. I didn't know for how long. I just knew my steady diet of cable news and commentary wasn't good for my soul. So I walked away.

After about six months of detox, I noticed that several things had changed in my heart and mind as a result of this (for me) significant life change. First, I no longer felt hopeless and defeated. I no longer thought the world was going to end or that "America, as we know it, will cease to exist." That's the ridiculous, never-ending chant from those who make their money from those who believe their rhetoric and keep coming back for more. (The truth is, America as we know it ceases to exist every day, and I'm okay with that. As we all contribute to solving problems and helping our fellow citizens, we continue to make America a different place.)

Second, I became less cynical toward politicians. I realized that many of them are hardworking Americans who love their country and are trying to do the right thing. It occurred to me that they need more of my prayers and less of my high-and-mighty criticism.

Third, I began to grow an appetite for hearing from people with whom I didn't agree. During my years as a news junkie, I lined up pretty well with most conservatives. When I consumed a steady diet of commentators telling me every night that "liberals" were evil, that they hated America, and that they were trying to take my kids and my freedoms and my rights, then I had no interest in sitting down with "those people" to hear what they believed, how they thought, what they valued, or what drove their worldview. I didn't want to hear it because I already knew. My favorite news personalities had told me it was true. But by shutting it off, I became more compassionate. I began to really care what people thought, even if I disagreed with them.

Finally, I became more interested in what Jesus would do than I was in holding the right political stance or what would happen in the next election. For example, when I look at illegal immigration through the eyes of Jesus and focus on how He would care for human beings who are trying to survive or find a better life, I land in a different place than when I think about it logically or economically or politically. If my filter is first loving God and loving others instead of making a point or winning an election or passing a law, then it makes a big difference in my life and in my attitude and focus.

Shutting off my excessive intake of cable news made me more loving, less tense, and more hopeful. I developed clearer thinking about real solutions for real problems, and my compassion for people around me began to increase. I began to want to know about other views and felt some of my own long-held beliefs shift as I released myself from the quicksand of groupthink. This will seem elementary to many, but I also discovered that Jesus is not a Republican and that "Christian" and "conservative" are not synonymous terms.

The bottom line is that this decision put me in a much better place. My soul is healthier and I am more kingdom-minded. I still love America, but I am more aware that Jesus died for the whole world, not just the USA.

For me, it was cable news that was making me less loving. For you, it might be a person who is pulling you into a cesspool of negativity. It might be an environment or a workplace. You may need to change what you read, watch, or listen to.

If you truly want to be a person marked by love, then remove the things from your life that keep you from being who you want to be.

3. Pray for a change of heart. I find it interesting how people use prayer. Many pray that they'll get the job, that they'll meet their sales goals, or that their car won't break down during the upcoming road trip.

I know that really smart pastors and theologians disagree with one another on weighty issues such as prayer and sovereignty and the work of God in our everyday lives. I tend to think pretty pragmatically about prayer, and that causes me to ask questions.

If God loves you so much that He gives you the job, does that mean He doesn't love other people who also applied and were praying just as hard? Do you think God supernaturally cleans your carburetor or patches the leak in your radiator?

I'm not saying God can't do those things. I'm just not sure that's where our prayers should be focused.

I'm more convinced that God wants to work in my heart, at a deep personal level, and that He can:

- Help me be more loving.

- Give me the strength to get through this tough conversation.

- Help me be more patient.

As I was mowing my lawn, instead of choosing to live in the cesspool of my own anger and bitterness, I began to pray. I prayed that God would change my heart. I prayed that I would become more loving. I prayed that I would stop obsessing about things that didn't matter. I prayed that I'd have opportunities to build a friendship with Tom. I prayed that God would help me become more loving.

And you know what? Before long, I stopped caring as much about that corner of my yard. Yeah, I still wished it was green and manicured. But more than that, I cared about Tom. I began looking for opportunities to express love in tangible ways to Tom and his family.

I don't know how prayer changes my circumstances or whether it does much to change someone else's. But I know prayer can change my heart. Because it has. And it does.

23
A WORLD OF "US VS. THEM"

B ack when America was just getting started, public shaming was the means to get people to behave. It was assumed that being humiliated in front of friends and family would keep people from doing the same crime again. And so, when you broke one of the enacted laws, you might be whipped in the public square, locked in stocks to be laughed at and have garbage thrown at you, or placed on a ducking stool and repeatedly submerged in a nearby lake.

According to the *Colonial Williamsburg Journal*, "Punishments were almost always public, for the aim was to humiliate the wayward sheep and teach him a lesson so that he would repent and be eager to find his way back to his flock."[38]

In the early 1600s, you could be punished if you failed to attend church services twice a day. The first offense would result in the loss of a day's worth of food, and the second offense would be a public whipping.

One guy who had been at sea for three years was punished for kissing his wife on a Sunday when he got off the ship. He spent several hours in stocks for his "lewd and unseemly behavior."

Aren't you glad you don't live in the 1600s? Society has advanced. We no longer stoop so low as to humiliate people for skipping church or for public displays of affection. We don't hang people in the streets. You can't go downtown to the city park to watch an execution. We are so civilized.

Or are we?

Since the beginning of the internet age, we again engage in public shaming, perhaps now more than ever. It's no longer a temporary punishment for a seemingly minor crime against society. Now you can be shamed for what you think, believe, or question, or even because you decide to start a business.

Consider the story of two young women who started making burritos out of a taco truck in Portland, Oregon. A local newspaper wrote a food review that sparked international outrage. Thousands of people left comments, many of them full of expletives and condemning words, for these young business owners. Because they brought their idea back from a trip to Mexico, they were accused of the "cultural theft of tortilla recipes" and branded under the category of "white supremacist." People angrily took sides, and within two days of the article, the owners had received multiple death threats and shut down their business out of fear for their own safety.[39]

In 2015, Walter Palmer, an American dentist and recreational big-game hunter, shot and killed a lion on a legal hunt in Zimbabwe. Little did he know that he had just killed Cecil the Lion, a well-known and loved attraction in the national park. Scientists and conservationists had followed and studied Cecil for many years. More than six million people viewed Jimmy Kimmel's emotional and impassioned mockery of the dentist. The public descended on Dr. Palmer, and within days he began receiving death threats. His home address was posted online, and he was forced to move his family and close down his dental practice for several weeks.

Internet shaming is a daily part of our lives now. Remember Adam Mark Smith? He was rude to a Chick-fil-A worker and then posted his verbal abuse on YouTube. He lost his job and had to sell his house and move to a new city.

Justine Sacco tweeted, "Going to Africa. Hope I don't get AIDS. Just kidding. I'm white!" It was a thoughtless thing to tweet. Little did she know that millions of people would be tracking her movements before her plane even landed. As the public humiliation mounted, she lost her job as a PR executive and eventually had to leave the country to find work.

The power of the internet combined with the ease of social media gives us the power to say something, and within a nanosecond it is distributed across the world. That same power means that when you speak without thinking, you can never get your words back. In an age of instant news and zero editorial oversight (everyone is a journalist), our words can cut deeper than any sword.

But it isn't just "the internet" that diminishes and bullies and demeans others. Sometimes it is you. And me. And we do it without thinking. And it has consequences.

We don't just debate ideas. We crush the people whose views don't line up with our own. We establish our position, we "hang out" with people who think like us, and then we attack those who disagree. It is "us" versus "them"—and we find energy in establishing our position and destroying people on the other side.

"Us versus them" sells. It creates headlines. There are entire news channels on TV and talk shows on the radio that make bazillions by pitting one group against the other:

- Republican vs. Democrat
- Liberal vs. Conservative
- Pro-life vs. Pro-choice
- Black vs. White
- Evangelical vs. Mainline
- LGBT vs. Traditional Family Values
- Red State vs. Blue State
- Homeschool vs. Public School
- The top 1 percent vs. the 99 percent
- Working Mom vs. Stay-at-Home Mom

This is the story of our planet. All around the world, for all of history, the us's have been killing the thems. Nazi Germany. Al Qaeda. ISIS. The Crusades.

But it's not just world wars or regional conflicts. It's not just news headlines and talk shows. Sometimes it is your Facebook page. Or your Twitter updates. Or your conversations with close friends.

This was perhaps not more apparent than in the 2016 United States presidential election. I watched my Facebook friends write some really harsh words:

No one who loves Jesus can possibly be voting for Donald Trump.

A vote for Hillary Clinton is a vote for killing babies.

In her book *Braving the Wilderness*, Brené Brown sums it up quite succinctly as she writes:

Here's what I believe:

1. If you are offended or hurt when you hear Hillary Clinton or Maxine Waters called b—, wh—, or the c-word, you should be equally offended and hurt when you hear those same words used to describe Ivanka Trump, Kellyanne Conway, or Theresa May.

2. If you felt belittled when Hillary Clinton called Trump supporters "a basket of deplorables" then you should have felt equally concerned when Eric Trump said, "Democrats aren't even human."

3. When the president of the United States calls women dogs, or talks about grubbing *%#&, we should get chills down our spine and resistance flowing through our veins. When people call the president of the United States a pig, we should reject that language regardless of our politics and demand discourse that doesn't make people subhuman.

4. When we hear people referred to as animals or aliens, we should immediately wonder, "Is this an attempt to reduce someone's humanity so we can get away with hurting them or denying them basic human rights?"

5. If you're offended by a meme of Trump Photoshopped to look like Hitler, then you shouldn't have Obama Photoshopped to look like the Joker on your Facebook feed.

There is a line. It's etched from dignity. And raging, fearful people from the right and left are crossing it at unprecedented rates every single day. We must never tolerate dehumanization—the primary instrument of violence that has been used in every genocide recorded throughout history.[40]

We have lost the ability to "agree to disagree." We have stopped treating people with the dignity every human being deserves. We don't seem able to discuss or debate a weighty topic without attacking the person who takes a position different from our own. For example, I recently heard a commentator debating deficit reduction say of the other side: "I wish they were all *%#& dead."[41]

That's strong. But it is symbolic of our culture. It is also symbolic of how we sometimes think about others. We might choose different words, but sometimes we just wish they didn't exist because:

- They don't think like I do.
- They don't see the world like I do.
- They don't treat people like I think they should.
- They don't stand for what's right like I do.
- They don't care about the poor as much as I do.
- They lack compassion.
- They care nothing about national security.

Jesus used harsh language at times. He occasionally got angry at people. But in every single case, His anger was toward those in His own camp—usually the religious leaders. His anger was because of how the "us's" were mistreating the "thems."

So how did Jesus treat the "thems"? How did He act

toward those who were not in His tribe?

Let's consider Zacchaeus. He was an outcast. He was both extremely well-known and extremely disliked. He was the guy who took money away from the poor and gave it to those who had plenty. He took money from his own kind, the Jews, and gave it to the occupying Romans. And for that service, he was rewarded well. And he also charged extra to pad his own pockets, so he was very wealthy. His wealth didn't come from hard work but from unjustly taking money from others.

Zacchaeus made his living by exploiting the helplessness of others. He cared only about himself. The Romans protected him, so the Jews couldn't hurt him personally. They could only hurt him relationally and socially by ostracizing him.

None of us loves paying taxes, but I don't think we look down on IRS employees like people in Jesus' day looked down on the tax collectors. Perhaps a better modern-day analogy is how most Americans view white supremacists. Most of us have little tolerance for people who mistreat others because of the color of their skin or their ethnic heritage. Zacchaeus was similarly considered the scum of the earth.

So how does Jesus act toward Zacchaeus? Does He mistreat him? Does He publicly humiliate him? Does He treat him with disdain or disgust? Does He write an open letter to the editor condemning his actions? Does He go on a tirade on Twitter, lifting Zacchaeus up as an example of what is wrong with the world?

He does none of that. In fact, He does something quite unexpected:

> *Then Jesus entered and walked through Jericho. There*
> *was a man there, his name Zacchaeus, the head tax*

*man and quite rich. He wanted desperately to see
Jesus, but the crowd was in his way—he was a short
man and couldn't see over the crowd. So he ran on
ahead and climbed up in a sycamore tree so he could
see Jesus when he came by.*

*When Jesus got to the tree, he looked up and
said, "Zacchaeus, hurry down. Today is my day
to be a guest in your home." Zacchaeus scrambled
out of the tree, hardly believing his good luck,
delighted to take Jesus home with him. Everyone
who saw the incident was indignant and
grumped, "What business does he have getting cozy
with this crook?"*

LUKE 19:1–7 MSG

Those who followed Jesus probably thought this was not His best moment. This was the guy pretty much everyone thought was the worst man on the planet. Not only did Zacchaeus take advantage of the poor, he did it for the enemy. And that made him one of the most hated men in the community. But Jesus publicly and loudly agreed to go to his house.

Jesus could have easily built a stronger bond with His followers by condemning this man. His followers would have cheered Him on if He had stopped to hurl accusations toward the greedy man in the tree. Instead, at great risk to His own reputation, He first offered to spend time with him.

And isn't it interesting that He doesn't just invite Zacchaeus over for coffee? He doesn't expect Zacchaeus to take the first step and come into His world. Instead, He makes the first move. He says, "Let Me come into your world."

This was so unexpected. It was countercultural. It actually may have been one of Jesus' *best* moments. It's the type of move no one expected, so everyone noticed. It's as though He was saying, "I know who you are. I know what you've done. I want to talk to you. I want to understand you."

Jesus moved into Zacchaeus's world. And by doing so, He was saying, "Your baggage, the way you've mistreated others, doesn't make you a lost cause. In fact, it makes you the most likely candidate for My love and grace."

And isn't that what we all want to hear?

It's what we want to hear from Jesus. But also from the people around us. It is what others want to hear from us. When we extend a hand, when we seek to understand and treat the unlovely with love and favor, we make inroads into that person's life.

I recently heard the story of a young woman who made this crystal clear for me. Read on. . . .

24
KILL 'EM WITH KINDNESS

Megan Phelps-Roper grew up in the shadow of West-boro Baptist Church. Well, that actually understates her involvement. From the time she was five years old, she stood in picket lines holding signs before she was even able to read them. Signs with words like "Gays Are Worthy of Death!" Their church website is GodHatesFags.com—and that should tell you everything you need to know about them. She parroted her parents and ten siblings as they combatted "evil" at baseball games and military funerals.

In a recent TED Talk, Megan talked about that time of her life: "We trekked across the country with neon protest signs in hand to tell others exactly how 'unclean' they were and exactly why they were headed for damnation. This was the focus of our whole lives."[42]

This fight continued as Megan grew up and began to lead the church's digital strategy. Most of the people she encountered online were as hostile and vitriolic as she had been taught to expect. So sides were established, arguments were made, and name-calling ensued. There was rage, scorn, criticism, and hate—and very rarely were any minds changed.

That is, until she crossed paths with some people who

were actually civil. They listened. They asked questions. They treated her with dignity and sincerely wanted to understand her perspective. Imagine that!

She said, "There was no confusion about our positions, but the line between friend and foe was becoming blurred. We started to see each other as human beings, and it changed the way we spoke to one another."

Eventually, Megan walked away from Westboro Baptist. And when she did so, she knew her family would never speak to her again. But in the most unlikely of places, she found people who loved and accepted her—even though they strongly disagreed with what she had believed in and preached her whole life.

Megan shared:

> We were shocked to find the light and a way forward in the same communities we'd targeted for so long. David. . .my friend from Twitter, invited us to spend time among a Jewish community in Los Angeles. We slept on couches in the home of a Hasidic rabbi and his wife and their four kids—the same rabbi that I'd protested three years earlier with a sign that said, 'Your rabbi is a whore.' We spent long hours talking about theology and Judaism and life while we washed dishes in their kosher kitchen and chopped vegetables for dinner. They treated us like family. They held nothing against us, and again I was astonished.

This is a clear example of the power of people who are marked by love. Love is the only antidote for the hate in our world. Someone who had been steeped for twenty years in intolerance and judgment had her eyes opened because of the way her "enemies" treated her.

But it's not just about the extreme views of Westboro Baptist Church. It's the world all of us live in. In her talk, Megan continued:

> *I can't help but see in our public discourse so many of the same destructive impulses that ruled my former church. We celebrate tolerance and diversity more than at any other time in memory, and still we grow more and more divided. We want good things—justice, equality, freedom, dignity, prosperity—but the path we've chosen looks so much like the one I walked away from four years ago.*
>
> *We've broken the world into us and them, only emerging from our bunkers long enough to lob rhetorical grenades at the other camp. We write off half the country as out-of-touch liberal elites or racist misogynist bullies. No nuance, no complexity, no humanity. Even when someone does call for empathy and understanding for the other side, the conversation nearly always devolves into a debate about who deserves more empathy. And just as I learned to do, we routinely refuse to acknowledge the flaws in our positions or the merits in our opponent's. Compromise is anathema. We even target people on our own side when they dare to question the party line. This path has brought us cruel, sniping, deepening polarization, and even outbreaks of violence. I remember this path. It will not take us where we want to go.*

Boom! That's it. Megan sums up the polarizing world we live in.

But here's the good news. We can actually do something about this. Love makes the difference. As we each strive to be marked by love, we can see the world change—one action, one response, one loving step at a time. We can listen better. We can find ways to find middle ground. We can work hard to see the topic we feel so strongly about through someone else's eyes.

This won't be easy. We all are convinced we are right! But if we want to be people who are marked by love, I suggest we work hard on these two disciplines:

1. Assume the Best

Seeing the best in others isn't natural for most of us. We typically project others' actions through our own filters. We want others to believe the best about our motives, while we tend to believe the worst about theirs.

Our brains naturally create a narrative about the behavior of others. When something bad happens—someone cuts us off in traffic, a friend stops reaching out, a coworker takes credit for our work—we instantly assume negative things about the other person. We assume we know his motivation, and we often ascribe ill intent with no real facts. Even though we've created this story in our minds, it quickly becomes real to us. And then we feel angry or hurt.

This happens at a subconscious level even in everyday interactions—and it happens in a flash:

- You see someone on Instagram who looks better than you in a swimsuit. You assume she had plastic surgery or he takes illegal bodybuilding supplements.

- Someone posts a picture of his new house. *I bet his parents gave them the money*, you think. *He doesn't have to work hard for his money like I do.*

- A friend expresses some views that are much different than your own. *I bet he's not even a Christian,* you may think.

We make stuff up when we are missing information. And for most of us, the story we create has a negative bent.

I suggest this: Start making up good stories. Choose to assume the best. Pick a mental narrative that minimizes your irritation and increases your compassion.

For example, when a guy pushes in front of you to get on the train, you might naturally think he's a selfish jerk who cares about no one but himself. *Or*, you could choose to assume he might be rushing home to an emergency situation.

And if your friend keeps letting your calls go to voice mail, instead of assuming he no longer wants you in his life, choose to believe he lost his phone.

This isn't about denying reality or living in ignorance of the world around you. It is merely assuming the people around you have the best intentions. It is choosing to bestow the benefit of the doubt on others—exactly the same you want from them. When it is someone with whom you disagree, you must intentionally decide to believe the best about that person.

Is someone as far away from you politically as the north pole is from the south pole? Don't assume he is in favor of the demise of your country. Choose to believe he has deep-seated values and cares greatly about people.

Did your boss just make what you deem to be the stupidest decision ever? Assume she has more information than you. Did your spouse just completely blow off your date night? Assume the best.

Did a friend just make a religious statement that is exactly the opposite of what you believe to be true about God or the Bible? Don't assume she has lost her faith.

If it helps, write "Assume the Best" on a card, and put it on your mirror or the dashboard of your car. Create a screen saver or wallpaper for your phone to constantly remind you to think the best of others. Put a sticky note on your computer screen to remind you to think before you speak out regarding a controversial topic.

Sometimes when I walk into an intense meeting or conversation I know is going to be fraught with conflict, I whisper over and over, "Assume the best. Assume the best. Assume the best."

Practice this until it becomes natural.

2. Seek First to Understand

If you are a student of Dr. Stephen Covey, you know this as the fifth habit of highly effective people.[43] And highly effective people are highly effective because they do things others don't.

If there were any way to take an accurate poll, I would guess it would reveal that 95 percent of us seek first to be understood. We want others to see things our way. We believe that if we just have a chance to say what we believe, then we will persuade others to move our direction. And yet others think the same, and so we end up talking over each other, neither of us caring that much about what the other is saying, or really even caring about one another.

Dr. Covey might have formed his thoughts from the Prayer of Saint Francis, first discovered in 1912. It says, in part:

> *O Master, let me not seek as much*
> *to be consoled as to console,*
> *to be understood as to understand,*
> *to be loved as to love.*[44]

In any confrontation, argument, debate, or controversy, go into the discussion intentionally looking to learn something you didn't already know. Look for ways to connect with the other person. By seeking first to understand someone, you communicate, "You matter. What you say has value. I may not agree, but I want to understand you better."

In Proverbs, a dad teaching his sons says it this way: "Wisdom is the most important thing; so get wisdom. If it costs everything you have, get understanding" (Proverbs 4:7 NCV).

Let's look at four practical skills you can begin practicing today as you seek to understand others:

Master the art of listening. To listen, you must stop talking and focus on what the other person is saying. I have a friend who has been working on becoming a better listener. He put a sign on his office wall, opposite his desk—he can see it just above the heads of those who come into his office to meet with him. It simply said: "WAIST." For most people, it has no meaning. But to him, it stands for "Why Am I Still Talking?"

Ask questions. Statements communicate how much you know. Questions tell the others that you value them and what they think. A few questions that work in just about every conversation:

How long have you had this view?

I can see you care very deeply about this—can you tell me more?

Get the person to tell his story. When you hear someone's story, you find out what makes him tick. You might learn that he is strongly against alcohol because of a personal tragedy involving a drunk driver. Or he may talk so openly about why parents shouldn't spank their kids because he was abused as a child.

Find out what the person values. When you ask questions and get others to share their stories, you learn about the values that drive them. Values are typically stored way below the surface. It might take many conversations before trust is built and you learn the core values that are the reason for their passion.

When we seek first to understand others, it has the effect of pulling the energy and emotion out of the conversation. Megan Phelps-Roper said it this way:

> *When my friends on Twitter stopped accusing and started asking questions, I almost automatically mirrored them. Their questions gave me room to speak, but they also gave me permission to ask them questions and to truly hear their responses. It fundamentally changed the dynamic of our conversation.*[45]

Proverbs says when we are kind to our enemies, it has the effect of heaping coals of fire upon their head (Proverbs 25:21–22). That sounds pretty aggressive. Perhaps a better translation is that it causes them to feel shame for the way they have acted. In essence, your kindness closes the gap between you and those you oppose.

Songwriter and musical sensation Selena Gomez was enjoying time on the beach with friends in 2015. Some photographers snapped a few photos, and pictures of her in a swimsuit were suddenly splashed across the internet. And people were not nice.

"Yeah, it was the first time I'd ever been called fat," Selena admitted. "But it was weird because it's not just, 'Oh, she's fat.' It's like, 'She's a mess. She's gone off the deep end.' I'm like, because I'm on a vacation wearing a bathing suit?"[46]

She admitted how deeply this hurt her. She considered how many of her young fans suffer bullying every day but have no platform to fight back. She responded by writing "Kill

'Em with Kindness." In the song's lyrics, she reflects on the cruelty of the world we live in and the harshness of the words so many carelessly launch toward others. She recognizes the impulse to fight back but encourages her listeners over and over to fight back with kindness.

Selena is right. You don't have to abandon what you believe. You don't need to lay aside your principles or your values. Just begin to treat others with civility and kindness. Become someone who is known for how you treat others with grace. Be a person who is marked by love.

Maybe I'm idealistic, but I really believe we can change the world, one gracious interaction at a time. It doesn't start somewhere else. It starts right here. With you. With me. Let's do this.

25
TESS RAN AWAY

What?" I replied.

My wife repeated, "Tess ran away."

"No she didn't. She's in the backyard," I said to Faith. Just a few minutes prior, I had let the dog out to do her thing in our fenced-in backyard.

"She's gone. She must have crawled under the fence."

Here's the deal: I didn't even like Tess. She was old and smelly and barked all the time for stupid reasons. In my contempt, I called her "Tessticles," mostly to make my wife laugh (how funny is it to yell out your back door, "Tessticles. . . time for dinner!"), but also to reiterate how much I didn't like this dog.

But I did like Roy and Judy. And Tess was their dog. We were only watching her for a few days while they were on a trip. Roy and Judy were at least eighty years old, and Tess was their life. I think it's actually possible they loved her more than their own grandkids.

So, when Tess disappeared under the fence, I knew they would be utterly devastated. We spent several hours that night walking around the neighborhood looking, calling her name, and asking neighbors and strangers if they had seen a small black (ugly) dog. As it got close to midnight, we gave up our search. Tess was gone.

We called Judy to let her know—in case someone might call the number on Tess's dog tag. Judy hadn't heard anything, but she said, "She's a house dog. . .why would you let her outside without a leash?" (Knife in our hearts.) "What were you thinking?" (Twist the knife.) Sobbing on the other end of the line. (Push it in, twist again.)

I had a hard time sleeping that night. We prayed for a miracle. I was mad at God. What kind of God would take a dog away from an elderly couple? It seemed mean and unnecessary.

I guess I eventually went to sleep, because the next morning I was awakened by an ugly, smelly dog licking my face. We have no idea how it happened, but Faith got up early and found Tess standing by our back door. Somehow, she had made her way back under the fence.

For the next several days, I replayed the emotions I felt during our twelve-hour crisis, and what it revealed about how I viewed God. Here are some of the questions I asked myself:

- Why did I so quickly get mad at God when Tess ran away?

- Why did I think God had anything to do with Tess leaving or coming back?

- In that moment, did I believe God was good because He brought Tess back? Or would I have still believed God is good if Tess had been found dead in the street?

- Do I somehow have more favor from God because this story had a happy ending?

I'd like to tell you I figured out the right answers to these questions. But to be honest, I didn't know the answers twenty-five years ago when Tess ran away, and I'm even less certain today than I was then.

One of the blessings of youth is having everything figured out—or at least believing you do. Freshman college students can be the worst, because they come home after a semester and have answers for everything. Until life happens, that is, and their perfectly crafted arguments begin to unravel.

I've spent thirty-plus years as an adult watching my own perfectly crafted arguments fall apart, one by one. I used to hold up certainty as attainable and a sign of maturity. Now I'm not so sure. The older I get and the more I study and experience life, the less I am actually sure about. *And I'm becoming comfortable with lack of certainty.*

Tragedy has a way of helping you come to term with your beliefs. Several years ago, Dr. Ben and Ann Witherington received news by way of a phone call that their thirty-two-year-old daughter had suddenly died in her home. Ben is a Bible scholar, professor of New Testament studies, and author of more than fifty books. He processed his grief in a blog, which became a booklet titled *When a Daughter Dies: Walking the Way of Grace in the Midst of Our Grief.* In a chapter called "Was This God's Will?" he addresses this question head-on:

> God did not do this to my child. God is not the author
> of evil. God does not terminate sweet lives with a
> pulmonary embolism.[47]

He goes on to describe the basis for his theology:

> I do not believe in God's detailed control of all events.
> Why? First, because I find it impossible to believe

that I am more merciful or compassionate than God.
Second, because the biblical portrait shows that
God is pure light and holy love. In him there is no
darkness, nothing other than light and love. Third,
because Job's words, "The Lord gave and the Lord has
taken away," do not express good theology!

There is so much I don't know about pain and suffering and evil and death. But even as there is less I'm certain about, there is one thing I believe more strongly than ever, and it's this: God is not the author of those things. God didn't cause the Holocaust, He didn't plan for ISIS to behead people on live TV, and He didn't dictate that young women would be pulled from their homes in the middle of the night and sold into sex trafficking.

God didn't make Tess run away any more than He caused your mom to die in a car accident or your baby girl to get a brain tumor. We live in an imperfect world. We are surrounded by pain and sickness and loss and disease and evil.

This became even more clear to me when my family received the worst of news in the winter of 2011.

26
HE GIVES AND TAKES AWAY.
OR DOES HE?

Every November, the Stevens Family celebrates *Thanksmas*. My brother, sister, parents, and all our families gather together—usually at my parents' home in Michigan—to celebrate a combination of Thanksgiving, Christmas, and several birthdays. It is three days of fun, laughter, and celebration.

On this particular Thanksmas, however, things took a turn for the worse. After we had opened Christmas presents, as was the custom on Friday morning, my sister pulled me aside and said, "You need to talk to Patrick. He's got some stuff going on, and it's really scary."

The next morning, I sat with my sister's husband, Patrick, at Big Apple Bagels near their home in Clinton Township, Michigan. Our family is close, so Patrick was more like a brother than a brother-in-law. He talked about physical symptoms that had begun to surface a few months prior. In the days we had just spent together, I hadn't noticed anything—except he didn't seem as jovial as usual. He had difficulty laughing, he explained, and could no longer pronounce certain words. He tried to say "Google" for me, but he couldn't do it.

He pointed to his arm and showed me how the muscles

were quivering nonstop. He had been searching online, looking for possible diagnoses, and it kept coming back as either amyotrophic lateral sclerosis (ALS) or a brain tumor. If he had to choose between those two, he said, he was hoping for a brain tumor. He had scheduled doctor visits and tests for the next week, so we agreed there was no reason to borrow trouble from the future.

A week later, on a Monday evening, my sister called to tell me the terrible news. The test results were 100 percent confirmed—Patrick had ALS. If his was a typical case, the doctors said, he would live two to five years. There is no known cure. It was devastating.

Two days later, I drove to Taylor University to tell my oldest daughter, Heather, that her uncle was dying, and then on to Detroit to hang with Patrick and Dena for the weekend. That Sunday morning, Patrick stood up in front of his church, where he had served as the youth pastor for twelve years, to tell the congregation that his days were numbered. Scores of students sat in the front rows of the church that morning, hearing for the first time that their youth pastor had a terminal illness. I still remember the shocked looks on their faces.

One of the songs we sang that morning was "Blessed Be the Name of the Lord." But I couldn't sing the part that says, "He gives and takes away...blessed be the name of the Lord." It was just too hard. I was standing by my sister, next to their kids, Paige (age eighteen) and Parker (age seventeen), and I still couldn't believe any of this was really happening.

For the next year, I drove four hours to Detroit every few weeks to be with Patrick and his family and help where I could. We set up a blog, organized fund-raisers, talked through finance and insurance details, and worked on quality-of-life projects. We joined them in April when he preached his final sermon. We watched people jump in to build ramps, widen doorways, renovate their bathroom, add stair railings, and provide wheelchairs, chair lifts, handicap vehicles, and more. Scores of people jumped in with donations and provided more than $75,000 to offset medical costs and to provide a college fund for the kids. It was amazing to behold.

But through all of the answers to prayer, I spent months internally dealing with my own denial and anger. I couldn't believe what was happening. I questioned why God would allow it. I didn't think He caused it (and I still don't, which is why I have a hard time with the song), but I knew He could have stopped it. So for months my question was "Why?"

- Why will my sister be without a husband at such a young age?
- Why will Paige and Parker be without a dad in such an important time in their lives?
- Why is the disease progressing so much more quickly with Patrick than with others?

My struggles with God's involvement in suffering came front and center one evening in May 2012. I had invited Ed Dobson to tell his story at my church.[48] Ed was at one time a pastor of one of the largest and fastest-growing churches in the country. He was also diagnosed with ALS, although his disease was progressing much slower than Patrick's. After the service, Ed and Lorna sat in our living room with Patrick and Dena.

That's when I heard Ed say, "If I thought God intentionally gives people ALS, I wouldn't be able to trust Him." Ed was a pastor, a seminary-trained preacher of the Bible. And as I watched these two men struggle to talk, unable to get off the sofa without help, and struggle to swallow every bite, he was saying the exact words I had been thinking.

Back to that song "Blessed Be Your Name," by Matt Redman. I'm okay with the verses, but the bridge does me in every time. It's a paraphrase from Job, a character in the Old Testament: "The LORD gave, and the LORD has taken away; blessed be the name of the LORD" (Job 1:21 ESV).

I can't sing it, because I don't believe it. I don't believe God gave Patrick ALS.

I recently heard of a pregnant woman struck by lightning—she was going to give birth the following week. She eventually recovered, but her baby died fifteen days later. I don't believe God directed that lightning bolt.

I once visited the hospital where a dear friend had just learned that her twenty-year-old daughter had a brain tumor. *She might lose her daughter!* I don't believe God put that brain tumor in her daughter's head.

I think about losing my mom, my sister, my brother, my amazing wife, one of our kids, or a good friend. I actually think about it a lot; it's probably my greatest fear. I don't wonder about God's sustaining grace or worry about the afterlife. I just hate the concept of death and don't want to lose those I love. I assume that is true of all of us to some degree.

When I say I don't believe that part of the song, I realize I'm saying that I don't believe a direct quote from the Bible. But those were Job's words, not God's, and they expressed his feelings. I respect that, but I just don't think the story or the Bible supports the accuracy of his words. It seems clear to me that God *allowed* all these bad things to happen to Job. He is sovereign and is in control, and Satan clearly had to get permission to mess with Job. But God did not *cause* them.

Dr. Ben Witherington explains it this way:

According to Job 1, it was not God but the Devil

who took away Job's children, health, and wealth.
God allowed it to happen, but when Job said these
words, as the rest of the story shows, he was not yet
enlightened about the true source of his calamity and
what God's will actually was for his life. God's will
for him was for good and not for harm.[49]

What kind of God would intentionally send children to their death through poverty and sickness? What kind of God would send a rapist into the home of a woman to terrorize her for hours? What kind of God would devise a plan in the hearts of men to fly jetliners into buildings filled with men, women, and children?

I realize that "His ways are not our ways" and that He is an infinite God. And I put my faith in that God. I don't need answers here on earth. I believe He will provide the grace to face anything that happens. I believe His love becomes more evident when we are facing difficulties (see Romans 8:35–39).

But I do not, and I cannot, believe that my God would intentionally give someone a horrendous disease.

So, what then is the *purpose* of suffering? I have no idea. I'm not sure there is a purpose. Purpose assumes intent. Some things just happen. The world is dark, and sometimes broken people inflict pain on others. Sickness exists, and sometimes people get sick. Freak accidents happen, and sometimes a person you love very much is here one minute and gone the next.

As a teen, I used to listen to Charles Swindoll's radio program every night on the radio. A quote I remember and still replay in my mind:

Life is 10 percent what happens to you, and 90 percent how you react to it.

That might seem to trivialize suffering or pain: "Oh, your mom just died? Well put a smile on your face and have a good attitude!"

I certainly don't mean it that way. Life really sucks sometimes. And there are times when you want to scream "Why?" toward the sky or bang your fists into your bed as you sob into your pillow.

Why? is a completely valid question. But there are other questions we can ask in the middle of suffering:

- Where is God's love more real to me now than before?

- How can I love this family as they face this tragedy?

- Where do I see unexpected and unexplained love or peace?

- How does this tragedy help me understand and love others better?

I remember when it shifted for me. Although given a life expectancy up to five years, Patrick died just a year after his diagnosis. About three months before he passed, my focus shifted. I got the chance to travel with Patrick and Dena to east Pennsylvania, where he had graduated college and seminary. They were giving him a lifetime achievement award. By this point, he could barely talk or stand. But the joy I saw him express to every person who stopped to greet him was—well, it was otherworldly. Watching him embrace his plight and do everything he could to brighten the lives of others. . .well, it flipped a switch inside of me.

I came back from that trip realizing how honored I was. I had a front-row seat to watch a man praise God until his dying breath. He was a prisoner in his own wheelchair, yet he did not curse God. He endured humiliating processes with the hospice nurse, yet still he chose to smile. He couldn't walk, scratch his nose, shoo a fly away, hold a pen, or speak a word. And yet he still chose to praise God.

Upon returning from that trip, I sent this letter to our four kids:

> I know you haven't been this close to someone dying before, and it is a tragic thing. But I want you to know how rare it is that someone dies like Uncle Patrick is dying. Many people have a difficult time living. Life can be overwhelming, and it is tough to do it with integrity and love. But as hard as living is, very few people die well. Some day in the next few weeks, Uncle Patrick will fall asleep and wake up in heaven. And he will be able to do so with a smile on his face and with no regrets. He didn't live a sinless life, but he lived a life of integrity. And even in his dying he is doing so with authenticity and vulnerability, while acknowledging his complete reliance on Jesus.
>
> As hard as this time is on all of you, I'm so glad we don't live a thousand miles away and you are able to experience it up close. He will be missed greatly, but we will all look back on his last days marveling at what a man of God he was all the way until the end.
>
> Life is fragile, and we never know when our next encounter with someone will be our last, so live a life with no regrets, giving your all to everyone who you hold close and dear.

When somebody is suffering, your role isn't to explain it. You can't fix it. You can't tell him why it is happening or when the pain will end. Your role, my role, is simply this: love. Do everything you can to lift the weight from that person's shoulders. Stand by your friend or family member all the way from the beginning to the end. Don't just love when it is popular and everyone is gathered. Don't just love in visible ways. Be the one who mows your friend's lawn or cleans his house when he can't get away from the hospital. Be the one to make a meal or fuel up his car or take care of his kids' college tuition.

Why do bad things happen to good people? I have no idea. Bad things happen to everybody. Hundreds of books have been written on the theology of suffering. Don't try to figure it out. Let the theologians argue about it. For you and me, let's just love each other a little bit more when the trials come. Let's hold each other up when everything is falling apart around us.

Remember—it's the very thing that sets us apart.

> *"By this everyone will know that you are my disciples, if you love one another."*
>
> JOHN 13:35 NIV

27
THE DAY I TRIED TO BUY A CAR

I was mad.

I had spent the previous three hours at the car dealership. I was leasing a new car, and they were doing the normal old-school tactics of coming in and out of the sales office, crunching numbers, saying "I have to check with my manager," and making me think I was getting the car for less than anyone had ever paid for a car in the history of the world.

Being the King of Research (I'm a 5 on the Enneagram. Anyone?), I had done my homework. By the time I walked in, I knew more about the car I was buying than the engineers who designed it. Well maybe not, but I definitely knew way more than the sales guy. I was spending my time educating him.

By the time I left the dealership, I felt used, humiliated, and demeaned. I had concern for every young buyer or single mom or "typical" customer who comes in not armed with the information I had—or the ability to negotiate. I have no problem with a business making money so it can stay in business. Nor do I have a problem with a salesman making money so he can provide for his family. But when that profit comes by dishonestly jacking up the numbers, by trying to hide profit, or through ridiculous add-ons I didn't ask for, and then making me, the customer, feel stupid or like a silly child who just doesn't understand adult things—I can't stand for that.

So, what did I do? I went home and posted my frustrations on Facebook. I didn't mention anyone by name, but I did mention the dealership and expressed my deep disappointment in its treatment of me as a customer. Several friends jumped on the bandwagon, and for a few hours we had a good time roasting this dealership by sharing actual customer experiences.

By that evening, I learned of many people I know who work for that dealership, including one of the owners. A few hours later, I received an email from a friend (let's call him Jack), who attended the church where I was a leader. Little did I know, Jack also worked for the dealership:

> Tim,
>
> I was deeply hurt and offended by your Facebook post today regarding your experience at (dealership). In my opinion, a better way to have handled the situation would have been to contact management at the store or our corporate office. By posting a very public message on Facebook, you demeaned not only my employer but also a salesman.
>
> Your actions and words today in my opinion were very toxic. As one of the leaders of our great church I was very hurt and disappointed by this public display.
>
> Ephesians 4:29 [NLT] states, "Don't use foul or abusive language. Let everything you say be good and helpful, so that your words may be an encouragement to those who hear them." Do you feel those words were encouraging to that salesman? Everyone makes

mistakes, Tim. I am certain the salesman did not explain things right and he was in the wrong for his actions. But your response on social media ridiculing him was also a mistake. I don't think attacking a salesman publicly is the way to win him to Jesus. As Christians, we should be speaking life-giving words, not toxic, life-taking words.

You are a person of tremendous influence, and your words today could be very damaging to our business and to the salesman.

Sincerely,
Jack

When I first read this letter, I didn't see his point. I wasn't foul or abusive. I didn't mention any names. I purposely didn't publicly question anyone's integrity or honesty (even though I personally questioned both). I merely shared my experience without commentary as to motives. I believed I was offering valuable insight to the public and feedback for the dealership's management. After all, how can a business get better and improve its practices without actual customer feedback?

And you know what? I was right.

But so was Jack. I deleted the posts.

As a follower of Jesus who is marked by love, I don't have the privilege of publicly airing my grievances, even if it is socially acceptable to do so. I am called to walk a higher road, to handle my frustration in a different way. If I want the world to be transformed by love, then I need to run my every conversation, email, tweet, and status update through a filter of love.

It's important here to make a distinction when it comes to issues of social injustice. There are times when people are being oppressed and love requires that we stand up and say something. When the rights of a fellow human being have been ignored or trampled, love compels us to use our place of privilege to link arms with others and say something. When the government enacts policies that disproportionately affect minorities, sometimes the most loving thing we can do is flip over tables like Jesus did and pronounce, "This isn't right!"

But so often our outrage is over having to wait too long in the checkout line, over suffering through a terrible ending to our favorite TV show, or over having our kids endure walking an extra block to the school bus stop because the administration made a change. We lash out in person or online with extreme words of shock and horror. We comment on the "idiots" who made the decision or created the piece of art we think is crappy. We question the motives of the politician with whom we disagree and draw extreme conclusions of how much he must hate our country.

We aren't left alone to figure out what it means to be loving with our speech. The Bible is full of wisdom about both the good and the potential harm we can do with our words. Most of us think about this in relation to the things you say with your lips, and that is important. But we also should reflect on the following verses as we to think about what we say online:

> "Be gracious in your speech. The goal is to bring out the best in others in a conversation, not put them down, not cut them out" (Colossians 4:6 MSG).

> "Words kill, words give life; they're either poison or fruit—you choose" (Proverbs 18:21 MSG).

> "A gentle response defuses anger, but a sharp tongue kindles a temper-fire" (Proverbs 15:1 MSG).

I'm certain most people don't realize the power of their words. We often use them carelessly and thus, we unknowingly hurt people.

I remember being interviewed in front of my choir in high school. The students could ask anything to get to know me as a new member in the choir. One of the upperclassmen raised her hand and asked, "Why do you have so many zits?" The class chuckled nervously, and I laughed it off. But thirty-five years later, I still remember it.

I'm 100 percent certain the person who spoke those words didn't intend to hurt me, and I'm pretty sure it didn't stick with her like it did with me.

Another time, when I was a young adult, a friend told me I had bird legs. He said, "It's not a bad thing, Tim. Just embrace it. There's nothing wrong with bird legs." Thanks! That really added value to my life.

The point of these stories isn't to make you feel bad for my former zitty-faced, bird-legged self. Rather, it is to remind you to consider the words you use—even with people you don't know.

Now that the words you "say" (i.e., tweet) about a celebrity or politician can be seen by that person the second after you send them, you have to consider your words. Would you say those same words to him in person or in front of his kids and family members?

We may think the acting in a recent movie we saw was awful, or that a certain singer's most recent album is the worst she's ever released, or that a politician is brainless and incompetent, but as a people marked by love seeking to transform the world, we must take the high road.

Whether you are talking to a friend, sending an email, or tweeting about a politician or entertainer, being marked by love means treating all people with dignity and respect, whether or not you think they deserve it.

We too easily swim in the stream of a culture that dehumanizes people we don't know. Here's what Brené Brown says about this in her recent book:

> Humiliation and dehumanizing are not accountability or social justice tools, they're emotional off-loading at best, emotional self-indulgence at worst. And if our faith asks us to find the face of God in everyone we meet, that should include the politicians, media, and strangers on Twitter with whom we most violently disagree. When we desecrate their divinity, we desecrate our own, and we betray our faith.[50]

Many preachers have used the following simple-to-remember acronym to make the point that we need to filter what we say (or type):

THINK Before You Speak:

T. . .Is it True?
H. . .Is it Helpful?
I. . .Is it Inspiring?
N. . .Is it Necessary?
K. . .Is it Kind?

For those striving to live as though they are marked by love, these are good questions to ask.

28
A STORY OF LOVE FROM
AN UNLIKELY SOURCE

Many Bible stories are really moving, and there is much to be learned from them. But the events portrayed in these stories happened thousands of years ago, so they can sometimes feel a bit intangible.

I get that Jesus looked up a tree Zacchacus had climbed and invited him to dinner. We already unpacked that story. The Good Samaritan story, which we talked about in an earlier chapter, is really cool. It's definitely a story of unexpected love. But it was also a parable—a made-up story to make a point.

Sometimes I need a really clear picture of unexpected love happening in front of me, in my space and time. Sometimes those stories make the biggest difference for me.

And sometimes they come from the most unexpected sources.

Sarah Silverman is an American comic. She is extremely talented and successful, but she is also known to be graphically crude and foul mouthed as she makes her points about sexism, racism, politics, or religion. She considers herself "godless" and "agnostic"—so she is not a person many

Christians typically look to as an example of how to become more like Jesus.

And yet, I recently saw in Sarah Silverman one of the purest examples of love I can recall. It brought tears to my eyes. It challenged me to do better, to be better, to love others better.

Silverman has a large Twitter following—more than twelve million receive her thoughts several times each day. She is a self-described liberal and had tweeted about an article where she tried to understand people who voted for Donald Trump.[51] I read the article she linked to, and I found that she wasn't at all unkind or dismissive. It seemed like she was truly trying to understand.

Yet one of her followers replied with one word, which I can't print here. It is one of the vilest, crudest, most offensive words in the English language. It is a terrible thing to say to anyone. It is degrading and devaluing. It's a word that says, "You have no worth. You are worse than scum. You are beneath me and everyone else."

Lashing out would have been defensible. Starting a social media campaign against the guy who said it wouldn't have been too far out of line. At the minimum, I would have blocked this person from my Twitter feed so I'd never hear from him again.

But instead of responding emotionally, Sarah Silverman followed the axiom "Seek first to understand." She looked back through this man's Twitter feed and learned that he was Jeremy Jamrozy and that he was in severe pain from debilitating back problems.

One hour after she received his terrible one-word reply, Sarah Silverman responded:

I believe in you. I read ur timeline & I see what

ur doing & your rage is thinly veiled pain. But u
know that. I know this feeling. Ps My back *%#&
sux too. See what happens when u choose love. I see
it in you.[52]

Sarah Silverman responded with love, understanding, empathy, and undeserved compassion. That, my friends, is the type of love that will change the world.

There is verse in the book of Proverbs that says, "A gentle response defuses anger" (Proverbs 15:1 MSG).

And that is exactly what happened with Jeremy. He responded to Sarah's loving and life-giving response, and he poured out his pain:

> *I can't choose love. A man that resembles Kevin Spacey took that away when I was 8. I can't find peace if I could find that guy who ripped my body who stripped my innocence I'd kill him. He @#$% me up, and I'm poor so its hard to get help.*

Silverman then replied with several more tweets acknowledging his pain and encouraging him to get help.

> *I can't imagine your rage. Just reading that makes me want to do bad things.*

> *All I know is this rage—and even if you could kill him— it's punishing yourself. And you don't deserve punishment. You deserve support. Go to one of these support groups. You might meet ur best bros there.*

Jeremy appreciated the advice:

I will go. But I trust no one. I've been burned so many times. I'd give the shirt off my back and everytime I get burned. I'm super antisocial. I have no friends. I'm sorry I gave u @#$%.

It has now been eighty-one minutes since Jeremy uttered that awful word toward Sarah Silverman—a person he'd never met and didn't know. When I say I believe love could change the world, it's in interactions like this where you can actually see it happening. One phrase, one response at a time, one decision to not lash out, one attempt to see things through the eyes of the other person.

Sarah graciously accepted his apology and again breathed life into Jeremy:

> *Dood I don't care. I'm fine. I see something in you. My gut tells me you could have a great life. My shrink says we don't get what we want, we get what we think we deserve. I'm telling you, you deserve so much more than you know.*

Jeremy's story isn't all that different from those of some of your friends, neighbors, work associates, acquaintances—or the hundreds of people you pass every week. Life sucks for a lot of people. Men and women have been abused and rejected and have never had anyone around them speak into their lives and say, "You have value. I can see something in you that is special. You are precious. I believe in you."

Those are powerful words.

If that is where the story ended, it would encourage and challenge me. It would make me wonder whose path I would cross that week, giving me the opportunity to have the same impact.

But Sarah Silverman went a step further. About four hours later, she leveraged her influence with twelve million followers and tweeted:

> *Yo San Antonio! Any @#$% back/neck care specialists willing 2 help my friend? He has several slipped discs, no insurance, and can't work bc of severe pain. Let's get him back on his feet!! Who's in?*

In a very short time, Sarah received responses from medical professionals willing to help. A week later, Jeremy was able to get an MRI showing he had five herniated discs. Sarah Silverman paid for the surgery to get Jeremy back on his feet.

Sarah put love into action. And this prompted love to come alive in Jeremy. He took some money he had raised and donated it to others for their health expenses. He said to mySanAntonio.com, "I was once a giving and nice person, but too many things destroyed that and I became bitter and hateful. Then Sarah showed me the way. Don't get me wrong, I still got a long way to go, but it's a start."[53]

Let me say it again: love makes a difference. You may not be able to pay for someone's back surgery, but everyone has the capacity to do something. Maybe you can sit with someone while he receives chemo treatments. Maybe you can offer to watch someone's kids so she can go to the doctor. Maybe you can look into someone's eyes and say, "I believe in you. I see you. You matter."

It's not going to be someone in the White House who changes the world. It's not going to be some new immigration policy or health-care solution either. The power doesn't reside in city hall or Hollywood or in a courtroom. You and

I have the power. It's in every word we speak. It's in how we value people. It's in the way we respond. It's in seeking to understand and see through the lens of another human being.

Love makes the difference. And it starts with my choice. And yours.

29
THE PASSENGER IN ROW 20

My return flight from Nashville was already running about an hour late, and everyone surrounding me at the gate was eager to get on the plane and get home. The flight was packed, so when the last person got on the plane and there were no seats available, the flight attendants became confused. From my aisle seat on row 9, I could see the pilots, flight attendants, and other airline officials looking at lists, walking on and off the plane, pointing, and talking some more. There was obviously a problem.

One passenger stood in the aisle. He had a boarding pass, but no seat. Soon, the announcements began:

> *"This is Southwest Airlines flight 699 going to Chicago. If you aren't going to Chicago, you should get off at this time."*

They repeated this announcement no fewer than ten times. Each time the words were said with more volume and emphasis. Then they started calling specific names: "If you are Jessica Klein, please raise your hand. If you are Bob Francis, please raise your hand." After about thirty minutes of calling names and begging anyone who wasn't going to

Chicago to get off the plane, there was still no movement.

This is where the Southwest Airlines "sit wherever you want" system officially broke down. Since there were no assigned seats, the flight crew had no way of knowing who was on the wrong plane. So the next step was to go through the plane, person by person, and check everyone's name off the passenger manifest. One official started at the front of the plane and another at the back.

Sure enough, somewhere around row 20, they found the offender. Turns out he was supposed to be on a plane to Columbus, not Chicago. How he was able to get on the plane with a boarding pass to Columbus, I have no idea. How he missed the multiple announcements about the destination of the plane, I'll never know.

But I do know what happened next. By now, we had been sitting on the plane for nearly two hours. We were going to be *very* late. The passengers around me were tired and many were agitated because they would be missing connections. So as the offender got out of his seat and gathered his belongings, the passengers jeered. They booed. They clapped as he took a walk of shame past twenty rows and left out the front of the plane. Some of them made sarcastic statements to him as he walked by:

"I guess you aren't going to Chicago with us?"

"Don't come back."

"Better get your hearing checked."

It was funny. I felt unified with the crowd. We were all experiencing the same emotions, and we finally had someone we could pin our frustrations on. But it was also sad.

I wondered what this middle-aged man (who looked like any other business traveler) was experiencing in his life to have been so zoned out during every announcement for the past hour. *Maybe his wife just died*, I thought. *Maybe he got fired earlier today. Maybe he learned his kid has terminal cancer.*

As the plane finally got in the air, I closed my eyes and reflected on the whole experience. I was troubled that I had been so easily sucked into the crowd's mocking vortex. I didn't participate, but I'm sure anyone watching me would have seen a man who seemed to enjoy how people treated this man. Honestly, I *did* enjoy it. But now, I could only think about the passenger from row 20. I breathed a short prayer for him.

I wondered how many Christians were seated around me. Jesus said we will be known by our love for others. But I'm not sure any of us on the plane that night would have been recognized as one of His followers. I know I fell short.

My two-hour drive from the airport would now get me home well past midnight, but I wasn't thinking about the late hour or the traffic or the city skyline. Instead, I kept thinking about the passenger in row 20. And I was thinking about my own heart.

I determined to do better next time.

And this is the frustration, isn't it? We do something unloving, and our action discourages us. We reflect on our judgmental thoughts, and they make us sick. We say something really mean to our spouse or kids or a close friend, and it discourages us almost to the point of wanting to give up.

But failure isn't failure unless you don't learn from it. From my lack of love for the passenger in row 20, all the way back to burying the bulldozer keys in the cornfield as a child—my reflections on my failures have convinced me that my life must be marked by love. Love continues to call me to a higher road, to a better way of living, and it is my failures along the way that motivate me to keep climbing.

Henry Ford said, "Failure is simply the opportunity to begin again, this time more intelligently."[54]

Nelson Mandela said, "Do not judge me by my successes, judge me by how many times I fell down and got back up again." [55]

And C. S. Lewis said, "Failures, repeated failures, are finger posts on the road to achievement. One fails forward toward success."[56] I honestly have no idea what a "finger post" is, but I get what it means to "fail forward."

The question is: What do we do? How do we start from where we are and become more loving? How do we begin to live differently?

I'll give you a bit of advice out of Alcoholics Anonymous tradition: "Just do the next right thing." Sometimes we see so many things we need to do that we feel paralyzed. So we do nothing.

You might feel overwhelmed at the number of people in your world with seemingly innumerable needs. You can't do it all. You can't fix all their problems. You can't love every person in the world. But you can *just do the next right thing*.

You may feel frustrated at the way you have treated others, the words you have carelessly let slip out, or the angry outburst that surprised even you. You may feel like you are burning relational bridges at every turn. You can't fix everything overnight. You likely won't be the person you want to be and know you can be in an instant. *Just do the next right thing*.

What is the next right thing? It's the first thing you know you can do and that you know will make a difference.

Let me suggest twenty-five places you can begin:

1. Pick a friend in crisis and find a way to meet one of his needs.

2. Consider your greatest bias or the people group you have a hard time understanding (rich people? another race? the LGBTQ community?). Find a way to enter that culture with the sole purpose of seeking to understand life from their perspective.

3. Stop praying for God to make your life easier, and instead pray that He will help make you more loving.

4. Make a friend of someone who is homeless, pause to hear that person's story, and do something to meet a need.

5. Find someone who believes the exact opposite of you in politics or religion. Take the time to build a relationship with him and ask questions until you can see the issue through his eyes.

6. Ask more questions. Make fewer statements.

7. Think of the family member you have the hardest time loving and then do something to show that person unusual and unexpected love.

8. Work on your budget so you have more margin to respond to the needs around you.

9. Talk less. Listen more. Ask lots of questions.

10. Pay for the car behind you in the drive-through.

11. Don't focus on sinning less; focus on loving more.

12. Choose to forgive someone, whether or not the person deserves it.

13. The next time someone attacks you in person or online, defuse the anger with a loving response.

14. Give your child's teacher a gift certificate to a restaurant just because she is awesome.

15. Begin to assume the best about the person you like the least.

16. Create margin in your schedule, and then begin to look for how you can love the next person you meet.

17. Do something random and anonymous for someone less privileged than you.

18. Stop trying to win arguments.

19. Seek first to understand.

20. Reread the chapters "Who Is My Neighbor?" and "The Principle of Proximity" and make a list of your neighbors. Then consider what you can do to begin loving them more.

21. Decide to never demean anyone or any point of view, online or in person.

22. Defend someone who is defenseless.

23. Start a GoFundMe.com page for someone who is in need and doesn't have the influence or network that you have.

24. Look for people who are marked by love and emulate them.

25. Speak life into someone—say the words "I believe in you."

This list as a whole might look overwhelming. Don't try to do all these—just pick one that speaks to you most strongly. Pick one you read and thought, *I could do that*. Then *do the next right thing*.

You may not be marked by love today. But do something loving every day, and pretty soon you might just start to look like a disciple.

30
YOU ARE LOVED

When our children were little, we had the book *Love You Forever*, by Robert Munsch.[57] The kids would consistently go back to this book when choosing their bedtime story. And when we were finished, they chanted, "Read it again, Daddy!" over and over.

Love You Forever is a story of a little boy who goes through the stages of childhood and becomes a man. Along the way, the most important thing he hears repeated is this simple refrain:

> *I'll love you forever,*
> *I'll like you for always,*
> *As long as I'm living*
> *my baby you'll be.*

The author originally published this as a children's book but was surprised when he learned how well it was selling in retirement communities. Adults were buying the book for other adults. Parents were buying it for their parents. And everyone was buying it for kids. More than fifteen million copies have been sold. And is there any wonder why?

You and I may not share the same skin color. We may not have grown up on the same side of the tracks. You might have grown up in church or maybe you've never set foot in one. You could be from Asia while I'm from North America. Whether we are gay or straight, man or woman, rich or poor, there is one thing we all have in common: we are all, every human alive, desperate to be loved.

I don't consider it too much of a leap to suggest that every addiction, every dysfunction, and every desire can be traced back to a craving to be loved. From our earliest days, we yearn for others to fully and completely and unconditionally accept us. We spend our childhood seeking this acceptance, first from our parents, then from our teachers and peers. To be fully known for all of our quirks and blind spots; to be fully accepted, even though we've messed up and hurt others; and to be fully loved through all of it—that is the core of what we live for.

We started the book talking about how Jesus was marked by love. When God looked down from heaven and spoke of His Son, at His baptism and then later toward the end of His life, both times He said, "This is my Son, marked by my love." He wanted to make one thing clear: God the Father fully loved Jesus.

And He wants to make something else clear as well: He loves you too.

Augustine said it this way, "God loves each of us as if there were only one of us."[58]

This may be a difficult concept for some. You may wonder, *How is it possible the God of the universe loves me? How can He accept me and think positive thoughts toward me when He, more than anyone, knows how unloving I can be?*

You aren't alone. I've sometimes been unable to believe that God can love me. Did He see what I just did? Did He hear what I just said? Does He know the thoughts that stayed far too long in my head? Of course He did and He does.

I think I question God's love sometimes because I'm so messed up by my own warped view of love. Others have disappointed me. I've experienced rejection. I've been in relationships that were great until I did something to mess them up. Relationships with others are often conditional, as in "I'll love you if. . ." or "I love you because. . ."

I remember trying to help my kids learn how to speak words of encouragement to others: "Tell your brother three reasons why you love him," I would say. I wonder, though, if I inadvertently taught them that love is earned.

But God's love for you and for me is different. It is otherworldly. It is beyond compare. It is not earned. It cannot be lost. In the New Testament, Paul says it this way: "But God shows his love for us in that while we were yet sinners, Christ died for us" (Romans 5:8 ESV).

Do you get the significance of this? Even when you refuse to forgive, even when you treat someone else like trash, even when you yell at your kids or steal from your employer, God still loves you. You may be bitter and negative and hard for another human to love—yet God is not fazed. Maybe it's been a long time since you've read your Bible and you long ago gave up on church. But that doesn't decrease God's love for you one bit.

In John's first epistle, he proclaims, "See what great love the Father has lavished on us, that we should be called children of God! And that is what we are!" (1 John 3:1 NIV).

You may not always feel it. You may not think you deserve it. But you are so loved. You cannot escape it. God loves you. There is no "He loves you because. . ." There is no "He loves you since. . ."

You are loved. Period.

John says, "We love because he first loved us" (1 John 4:19 NIV). It is His love that gives us the capacity to love others. The more we fully accept and embrace God's love for us, even with all our flaws, the more we are fully able to love others, even with all their flaws.

Jesus was marked by God's love. I don't think it's a coincidence that His life mission was all about helping people become more loving.

31

IT'S THE ONLY THING THAT MATTERS

Have you noticed a common thread throughout the life of Jesus?

In Jesus' final words to His disciples, He makes a speech that is thirty-five words long, and three times He repeats: "Love one another." He says His disciples will be known by their love for one another. They won't be known by their sermons, how much they know, or whether they follow the rules or read the Bible. They will be known by whether they are marked by love. That is it.

Another time, when Jesus is asked about the most important commandment in the Bible, without hesitation He says we are to "love God and love others." He essentially says, "All of Scripture does not have equal weight. If you do nothing else, love God and love others." There is nothing else more important than love.

When Jesus meets the harlot, He doesn't condemn her or ignore her or cast her out. Instead, He celebrates her acts of love toward Him and tells the religious leaders nearby that they have much to learn from this woman.

In the story of the Good Samaritan, Jesus teaches that

love transcends the societal barriers of race, gender, culture, and religion. We are to love those who look like us and those who don't. We are to love those who are hard to love, even when it inconveniences our schedule or lifestyle.

Another time, He goes one more step and challenges us to love our enemies. Not from a distance either. He says if our enemy is hungry, feed him; if he needs something like a new coat, go buy it for him.

You might say, "But Jesus doesn't know my enemies and the hurt they've caused me!" Has anyone run a spear through your side? I think He understands.

When Jesus publicly invites Himself to Zacchaeus's house for dinner, He ignores all the cultural do-not-cross lines of His time. He shows the world that the only way to move beyond our biases and judgmental hearts is to enter someone else's world, seek to understand life through that person's eyes, and extend a hand of love. Don't wait for that person to come your direction. Love compels you to enter his world.

I realize this whole book may come off as one big cliché:

> *Let's just all take off our shoes, touch toes, sit around a campfire, and sing Kumbaya.*

> *Can't we all just get along?*

> *Love makes the world go 'round.*

You might be thinking that I have way oversimplified the world. *Really, love is the only thing that matters?* you may be asking. *Life is more complicated than that, Stevens. Wake up and stop smelling the roses.*

I get that life is messy and bloody and sometimes violent. I understand that sometimes you need to fire an employee, evict a tenant, or draw a line in the sand with your teenager. Sometimes you have to make tough decisions.

But even those hard decisions can be run through a filter of love. Setting healthy boundaries does not mean you are unloving. It's not about the decision you have to make or position you have to take but about how you communicate, about treating people with dignity, about respecting people with opposing opinions, about showing love and compassion through every step.

I may be naive, but I have to believe that lack of love is at the source of. . .

- The Las Vegas musical festival shooting
- The nuclear tension between North Korea and the United States
- The constant fights in Congress and refusal to find middle ground
- Violence in our inner cities
- Domestic and sexual abuse
- Racial injustice
- Human trafficking
- Online verbal assaults
- Church splits
- Your most recent family argument
- Every conversation containing gossip or slander

Can you tell me it wouldn't make a difference if the people involved in each of these events or actions had been marked by love?

We can't change the world. Not by ourselves. But we can

change *our* world. We can each make a difference within our circle of influence.

One of the best-known and oft-quoted Bible passages is 1 Corinthians 13. This chapter has been the source of content for blockbuster songs and speeches by presidents and kings, and it has been printed countless times on posters, artwork, and memes.

And so, I end this book with the words of the apostle Paul to a church struggling to get along and make things work in their small community of faith. It's the struggle all of us face, to some degree, in each of our circles. We have much to learn. So here it is, along with my own commentary in italics:

1 Corinthians 13 (NLT)

"If I could speak all the languages of earth and of angels, but didn't love others, I would only be a noisy gong or a clanging cymbal."

> *It doesn't matter how smart you are, without love you are just making noise when you speak.*

"If I had the gift of prophecy, and if I understood all of God's secret plans and possessed all knowledge, and if I had such faith that I could move mountains, but didn't love others, I would be nothing."

> *You might be a really good preacher. People might come from all over to hear you talk or seek wisdom from you. You might be a strong person of faith. But none of that matters if you don't love others.*

"If I gave everything I have to the poor and even sacrificed my body, I could boast about it; but if I didn't love others, I would have gained nothing."

> *It doesn't matter if I give 90 percent of what I earn to charity. It doesn't matter if I would stand in front of a train to save a village. If I haven't been marked by love in my everyday words, thoughts, and actions, I have missed the point.*

"Love is patient and kind. Love is not jealous or boastful or proud or rude. It does not demand its own way. It is not irritable, and it keeps no record of being wronged."

> *If I live my whole life and only work on these four sentences, then I have my work cut out for me. This is where being "marked by love" gets tangible. Am I known to be patient and kind? Am I humble, or do I always want to point out my accomplishments to others? Do I sometimes demand to get my way? Do little things annoy me to the point of affecting the happiness of others around me? Do I keep track of wrongs done against me? I have a lot of work to do here.*

"It does not rejoice about injustice but rejoices whenever the truth wins out."

> *How does being marked by love impact my view on solving the homelessness crisis? What about immigration? Do I fight against injustice and celebrate when a court case finally proves the systemic abuse by those in power toward those who aren't? Love compels me to speak up for those who can't.*

"Love never gives up, never loses faith, is always hopeful, and endures through every circumstance."

How does this work when everything is stacked against me? What does it mean to be marked by love when I am being abused or held down? I have much to learn from those who have been imprisoned but have kept their hope alive, faith strong, and love enduring.

"Prophecy and speaking in unknown languages and special knowledge will become useless. But love will last forever!"

When I choose to love someone, it has ripple effects into eternity. If I make a speech, the impact will last for a few minutes, maybe a few hours, perhaps even several decades if it's really inspired. But when I live a life marked by love, it affects everyone around me—those closest to me as well as people who will never know my name. It changes how I do life with my family and how I raise my children. It literally has immeasurable eternal consequences.

"Now our knowledge is partial and incomplete, and even the gift of prophecy reveals only part of the whole picture! But when the time of perfection comes, these partial things will become useless."

There are things way too complicated for me to understand or see. But love is not complicated. And it lasts.

"When I was a child, I spoke and thought and reasoned as

a child. But when I grew up, I put away childish things. Now we see things imperfectly, like puzzling reflections in a mirror, but then we will see everything with perfect clarity. All that I know now is partial and incomplete, but then I will know everything completely, just as God now knows me completely."

> *Stuff will happen in this life I will never understand. Wars begin. Families fight. Kids die of starvation. The world is a difficult place, and I can't fully understand it. It will make sense someday. But for now. . .*

"Three things will last forever—faith, hope, and love—and the greatest of these is love."

> *. . .I focus on what I can understand and control. Faith is really important. Knowing what I believe and why I believe it matters. And confidence that tomorrow can be better is a really good thing.*
>
> *But more than faith, more than hope—the greatest attribute of all is love. It's the only thing that matters.*

NOTES

NOTES

1. Statistics Brain Research Institute, "Tattoo Statistics," accessed May 22, 2018, http://www.statisticbrain.com/tattoo-statistics/.

2. Meredith Bennett-Smith, "Rouslan Toumaniantz, Tattoo Artist, Inked Name Across Girlfriend Lesya's Face, Hours After They Met," *HuffPost*, December 6, 2017, http://www.huffingtonpost.com/2013/02/04/rouslan-toumaniantz-girlfriend-face-tattoo_n_2617994.html.

3. Carnegie Mellon University, "Randy Pausch Last Lecture: Achieving Your Childhood Dreams," YouTube, December 20, 2007, https://www.youtube.com/watch?v=ji5_MqicxSo.

4. This final sermon, along with ten other sermons Patrick preached in his final few years on this earth, were recently published in a book in his honor: *Who Do You Trust? A Compilation of Sermons by Patrick D. McGoldrick*. Available at http://amzn.com/1482634988.

5. Patrick D. McGoldrick, "A Year Ago….," *Patrick's Story* (blog), December 5, 2012, patricksstory.wordpress.com/2012/12/05/a-year-ago.

6. Pam Butler, "Hard Decisions," *Always on the Sunny Side* (blog), February 26, 2013, http://alwaysonthesunnyside.wordpress.com/2013/02/.

7. This study was published in David Kinnaman and Gabe Lyons, *unChristian: What a New Generation Really Thinks About Christianity…and Why It Matters* (Grand Rapids, MI: Baker, 2012), 29–30.

8. Paul Schankman and Vera Culley, "Local Pastor Alois Bell's Tip, 'I Give God 10%' Gets Applebees Waitress Fired," Fox2Now, February 1, 2013, http://fox2now.com/2013/01/31/web-world-i-give-god-10-receipt-goes-viral/.

9. Susan K. Smith, "Christians Give God a Bad Name," *OnFaith*, July 15, 2008, https://www.onfaith.co/onfaith/2008/07/15/christians-give-god-a-bad-name/61.

10. Audrey Barrick, "Study: American, Christian Lifestyles Not Much Different," *Christian Post*, February 6, 2007, http://www.christianpost.com/news/study-american-christian-lifestyles-not-much-different-25642/.

11. Caroline Gavin, "Jesus, Since I Met You," Heartstone Journey, July 15, 2012, http://heartstonejourney.com/jesus-since-i-met-you/.

12. "Leprosy Overview," WebMD, accessed May 22, 2018, http://www.webmd.com/skin-problems-and-treatments/guide/leprosy-symptoms-treatments-history#1-3.

13. It's an interesting side note that in most these cases, the people completely disobey Jesus' instructions and tell everyone they know what just happened. That's a whole theological can of worms, but is it possible that Jesus is less concerned about our words about Him and more concerned about our hearts for Him and the people He created? Put that in your pipe and smoke it!

14. "The Facts and Stats on 33,000 Denominations," Philvaz.com, accessed May 22, 2018, http://www.philvaz.com/apologetics/a106.htm.

15. Check them out in Sarah Nelson's article "#MCM: Alex Radelich of Explore Kindness," *Anna* (online magazine), April 30, 2017, http://www.annathemag.com/home/2017/4/30/mcm-alex-radelich.

16. Lewie Clark's ministry is called Icon Ministries. Check them out at http://imitatingjesus.org/about-icon/.

17. C. S. Lewis, *Mere Christianity* (New York: MacMillan, 1952).

18. "Pornography Report: 2015 Statistics," Covenant Eyes, accessed May 22, 2018, http://www.covenanteyes.com/pornstats/.

19. Mark Barna, "Focus Puts Retailers on Naughty and Nice List for Christmas," *The Gazette*, November 14, 2008, http://www.gazette.com/articles/christmas-43437-focus-retailers.html.

20. Some of this history found here: Wikipedia, s.v. "Christmas Controversies," accessed May 22, 2018, http://en.wikipedia.org/wiki/Christmas_controversies.

21. Herb Silverman, " 'War on Christmas': A Holiday Tradition for All," *Washington Post*, December 11, 2012, https://www.onfaith.co/onfaith/guest-voices/the-war-on-christmas-a-holiday-tradition-for-all.

22. Russell D. Moore, "Is the Culture at War with Christmas?," *Christian Post*, December 9, 2012, http://www.christianpost.com/news/is-the-culture-at-war-with-christmas-86306/.

23. You can watch the film *Our Road* to hear Gene tell his story of grace and recovery; http://findyouropenroad.com.

24. John Ortberg, "Who Is My Neighbor?" (sermon, Menlo Park Presbyterian Church, Menlo Park, CA, November 13, 2013), http://mppc.org/series/who-my-neighbor/john-ortberg/who-my-neighbor.

25. William Lobdell, "An Amazing Act of Forgiveness," *Los Angeles Times*, October 9, 1999, http://articles.latimes.com/1999/oct/09/local/me-20503.

26. Melanie Curtin, "This 75-Year Harvard Study Found the 1 Secret to Leading a Fulfilling Life," Inc.com, February 27, 2017, https://www.inc.com/melanie-curtin/want-a-life-of-fulfillment-a-75-year-harvard-study-says-to-prioritize-this-one-t.html.

27. Jonathan Potts, "Happy People Are Healthier, Carnegie Mellon Psychologist Says," Carnegie Mellon University, accessed May 23, 2018, https://www.cmu.edu/news/archive/2006/november/nov.-6-happy-is-healthier.shtml.

28. Janice K. Kiecolt-Glaser et al., "Hostile Marital Interactions, Pronflammatory Cytokine Production, and Wound Healing," *JAMA Psychiatry* 62, no. 12 (2005), https://jamanetwork.com /journals/jamapsychiatry/fullarticle/209153.

29. Kirsten Weir, "Forgiveness Can Improve Mental and Physical Health," *Monitor on Psychology* 48, no. 1 (2017): 30, http://www .apa.org/monitor/2017/01/ce-corner.aspx.

30. Paul Singer, "Faith Groups Provide the Bulk of Disaster Recovery, in Coordination with FEMA," *USA Today*, September 10, 2017, https://www.usatoday.com/story/news /politics/2017/09/10/hurricane-irma-faith-groups-provide-bulk-disaster-recovery-coordination-fema/651007001/.

31. Raj Raghunathan, "The Need to Love: One of the Best Kept Secrets of Happiness Is to Love and Take Care of Others," *Psychology Today*, January 8, 2014, https://www.psychologytoday .com/blog/sapient-nature/201401/the-need-love.

32. *Merriam-Webster*, s.v. "stereotype (n.)," accessed May 23, 2018, http://www.merriam-webster.com/dictionary/stereotype.

33. *Merriam-Webster*, s.v. "generalization (n.)," accessed May 23, 2018, http://www.merriam-webster.com/dictionary /generalization.

34. John Piper, "Stereotypes, Generalizations, and Racism," Desiring God, January 17, 2007, http://www.desiringgod.org /resource-library/taste-see-articles/stereotypes-generalizations-and-racism.

35. "Theodore Roosevelt," Goodreads.com, accessed May 23, 2018, https://www.goodreads.com/quotes/34690-people-don-t-care-how-much-you-know-until-they-know.

36. Richard Swenson, *Margin: Restoring Emotional, Physical, Financial, and Time Reserves to Overloaded Lives* (Colorado Springs, CO: NavPress, 2004), 69.

37. Kary Oberbrunner, "15 Reasons Why You Need Margins in Your Life," *Kary Oberbrunner Igniting Souls* (blog), accessed June 22, 2018, https://karyoberbrunner.com/blog-home/blog-purpose/15-reasons-why-you-need-margins-in-your-life.

38. James A. Cox, "Bilboes, Brands, and Branks: Colonial Crimes and Punishments," *Colonial Williamsburg Journal* (Spring 2003), http://www.history.org/foundation/journal/spring03/branks.cfm.

39. Matthew Korfhage, "The Battle Over Kooks Burritos Led to Death Threats and International Outrage," *Willamette Week*, June 6, 2017, http://www.wweek.com/restaurants/news-restaurants/2017/06/06/the-battle-over-kooks-burritos-led-to-death-threats-and-international-outrage-we-invited-portland-chefs-to-weigh-in/.

40. Excerpt(s) from BRAVING THE WILDERNESS: THE QUEST FOR TRUE BELONGING AND THE COURAGE TO STAND ALONE by Brené Brown, copyright © 2017 by Brené Brown. Used by permission of Random House, an imprint and division of Penguin Random House LLC. All rights reserved.

41. Dan Savage, "I Wish They Were All [redacted] Dead," YouTube, July 19, 2011, https://www.youtube.com/watch?v=fPgPxx_HVCU.

42. Megan Phelps-Roper, "I Grew Up in the Westboro Baptist Church. Here's Why I Left," TED.com, accessed May 23, 2018, https://www.ted.com/talks/megan_phelps_roper_i_grew_up_in_the_westboro_baptist_church_here_s_why_i_left/transcript.

43. "The Seven Habits of Highly Effective People: Habit 5; Seek First to Understand, Then to Be Understood," FranklinCovey.com, accessed May 23, 2018, https://www.franklincovey.com/the-7-habits/habit-5.html.

44. Wikipedia, s.v. "The Prayer of St. Francis," last modified May 15, 2018, https://en.wikipedia.org/wiki/Prayer_of_Saint_Francis.

45. Megan Phelps-Roper, "I Grew Up in the Westboro Baptist Church. Here's Why I Left."

46. Antoinette Bueno, "Selena Gomez on Being Fat Shamed: My Bikini 'Was A Little Too Small' for Me, But I Didn't Care," ETonline.com, October 9, 2015, http://www.etonline.com /news/173674_selena_gomez_talks_being_being_fat_shamed_to_ ellen_degeneres.

47. Ben Witherington and Ann Witherington, *When a Daughter Dies: Walking the Way of Grace in the Midst of Our Grief* (Carol Stream, IL: Christianity Today, 2012), loc. 94 of 794, Kindle.

48. You can read more about Ed's story at http://edsstory.com/. He was diagnosed in 2000, lived for fifteen years with the disease, passing away in late 2015.

49. Witherington, *When a Daughter Dies*, loc. 94 of 794.

50. Excerpt(s) from BRAVING THE WILDERNESS: THE QUEST FOR TRUE BELONGING AND THE COURAGE TO STAND ALONE by Brené Brown, copyright © 2017 by Brené Brown. Used by permission of Random House, an imprint and division of Penguin Random House LLC. All rights reserved.

51. Jeremy Jamrozy (@Jeremy_Jamrozy), Twitter, December 28, 2017, 4:35 p.m., https://twitter.com/jeremy_jamrozy /status/946540038619312129.

52. Sarah K. Silverman (@SarahKSilverman), Twitter, December 28, 2017, 5:36 p.m., https://twitter.com/SarahKSilverman /status/946555534768979969.

53. Madalyn Mendoza, "Once A Troll, San Antonio Man Uses New Friendship with Sarah Silverman to Help Others," mySanAntonio.com, January 3, 2018, https://www.mysanantonio .com/lifestyle/article/S-A-man-who-once-trolled-Sarah- Silverman-now-12471548.php#photo-14787255.

54. "Henry Ford Quotes," BrainyQuote.com, accessed May 23,

2018, https://www.brainyquote.com/quotes/henry_ford_121339.

55. "Nelson Mandela," Goodreads.com, accessed May 23, 2018, https://www.goodreads.com/quotes/270163-do-not-judge-me-by-my-successes-judge-me-by.

56. "C. S. Lewis Quotes," BrainyQuote.com, accessed May 23, 2018, https://www.brainyquote.com/quotes/c_s_lewis_119178.

57. Robert Munsch, *Love You Forever* (Buffalo, NY: Firefly Books, 1995).

58. "Beliefnet's Inspirational Quotes," beliefnet.com, accessed May 23, 2018, http://www.beliefnet.com/quotes/christian/s/st-augustine/god-loves-each-of-us-as-if-there-were-only-one-of.aspx.

MORE GOOD NEWS FOR A TIME AND CULTURE THAT DESPERATELY NEED IT

#Gospel by Daniel Rice

Through current cultural references and true stories, Daniel Rice, founder of #Gospel LLC, will help readers come to see the gospel for what it really is and how it can radically alter their everyday lives. Rice invites them into the conversation as he breaks down Paul's explanation of the Gospel in Romans in a way that is accessible and engaging. *#Gospel*. . .good news for a time and culture that desperately need it.

To see relevant videos, visit www.HashtagGospel.com

Paperback / 978-1-68322-477-8 / $14.99